FROM A PERSIAN KITCHEN

AUTHENTIC RECIPES & FABULOUS FLAVOURS FROM IRAN

FROM A PERSIAN KITCHEN

RECIPES & PHOTOGRAPHY BY
ATOOSA SEPEHR

ROBINSON

I would like to dedicate this book to my parents, Maryam and Daryoush and to my grandmother Nahid and aunt Lili, who have always supported me and encouraged me to do the things that make me happy.

I would also like to thank my best friend Brian, who is a constant source of inspiration.

Flower Man, Isfahan, Iran (April 2017)

CONTENTS

Introduction	8
Persian Ingredients & Techniques	12
Mezze, Starters & Sides	22
Salads	48
Kookoo & Kotlet	70
Soups	88
Rice	110
Stews	138
Kebabs, Roasts & Grills	170
Bread, Pizza & Pasta	198
Desserts & Drinks	216
Index	237

INTRODUCTION

In Iran, everything is about food, and people take great pride in the dishes they prepare, offering at least two or three at every meal. Growing up in Iran I took all this for granted. My mom is an amazing cook and was always very particular about using the best ingredients, even if it meant driving out of the city to the farms or village markets on the outskirts of Isfahan to get the ingredients she needed. This meant that we always had good food on our table.

I was born in the city of Shiraz in south-central Iran, but at the age of four I moved with my family to Italy, where my father worked for several years as an engineer in the cities of Genoa, Massa and Reggio Emilia. We all enjoyed the new flavours that Italian cooking offered. After that, discovering new kinds of food and experimenting with cooking became a big part of the way I experience each new country I visit.

When we returned to Iran, I rediscovered the pleasures of traditional Persian food. I spent the rest of my childhood and teenage years in Isfahan in central Iran, and when I left Isfahan to attend university in the city of Tabriz (north-west Iran), without my mom to cook for me, I began to recreate her dishes for myself. Soon, I was cooking for all my friends, and making and sharing food became an important part of the community we formed; I would cook and we would talk about our studies, our lives and our futures. For me, eating Persian food has always been a social act, a coming together of the people I love, enjoying a meal in each other's company.

Going out into the real world after university meant there was less time for cooking. After completing my MBA I worked in the import and export business in Tehran, eventually establishing my own company. Life wasn't always easy and I missed the simple sense of happiness that cooking gave me and so I decided that something needed to change. In 2007, I relocated to London, working for an Iranian steel company while studying for my ACCA accountancy qualification. I have never felt so welcome anywhere as I have in London and it is a place where I feel truly at home. When I became a British citizen in 2014 it was one of the proudest moments of my life. It is a real privilege to live in the great city of London and I feel compelled to give something back to my adopted country by sharing my love of Persian cooking.

I was first inspired to write this cookbook after a summer party at my home in London. There were approximately 60 guests, most of whom grew up in Europe and the US and had not tasted Persian food before. I served mostly Persian food because I wanted to introduce my friends to the cuisine of my country. Both during and after the party, my guests commented on how wonderful the Persian food was, with its astonishing range of flavours and textures. Some of them requested recipes and after a few months I had compiled a collection of recipes, many of which have made their way into this book.

What makes Persian cuisine so special is the variety and combinations of ingredients, including spices, fresh and dried herbs, saffron, rose water, aubergines, dried fruits and nuts. The history of Persian cooking can be traced back to the sixth century BC, when Cyrus the Great established the first Persian empire. At its height, the empire stretched from India to Egypt and parts of Greece. Persian ingredients, such as saffron and rose water, spread throughout the lands of this vast empire. Persians also conducted trade with the kingdoms of the Far East; caravans travelling along the

Silk Road from China to present-day Syria brought not just silks, but also spices, citrus fruits, aubergines and rice from Asia to the Middle East. When I cook Persian food, I feel a sense of connection to this long and fascinating history and I take comfort in knowing that despite changing geographical and political boundaries, Persian cuisine has survived and thrived, and is increasingly enjoyed in the west.

In this book, I have included many of the most popular Iranian dishes and some of my own personal favourites. The recipes reflect regional differences, from the garlic, fresh herbs and pomegranate molasses of northern Iran by the Caspian Sea to the spicier palate of the south. Many recipes combine Persian rice, lamb, chicken or fish with a wide variety of herbs. There are also plenty of dishes suitable for vegetarians. I have tried to make the recipes as authentic as possible, but I am aware that certain ingredients, such as *kashk* (a thick white dairy product with a strong umami flavour), can be difficult to find in the UK and I have suggested alternatives.

The recipes are organized into nine sections: **Mezze, Starters and Sides** is a collection of small dishes that can be served singly or as mixed *mezze*, where three or more dishes are served together as an attractive appetizer; most of the **Salads** could also be served as starters or side dishes; **Kookoo and Kotlet** covers some of Iran's best-loved egg-based dishes; Persian **Soups** are substantial affairs that make a meal in themselves, rather than being served as a first course; there is a huge variety of **Rice** dishes in Iranian cuisine – their distinguishing feature is the *tahdig*, the delicious crispy layer that forms at the bottom of the pan; **Stews** are typically slow-cooked dishes based on lamb or chicken, often combined with fruit, vegetables or herbs; **Kebabs, Roasts and Grills** are some of Iran's most popular dishes; Persian **Bread, Pizza and Pasta** have their own unique personalities; and the **Desserts and Drinks** are subtle and scented.

When I began working on this book I decided to style and shoot all the photographs myself. Drawing on my lifelong love of still-life painting helped me to capture the wonderful textures of Persian food as well as the atmospheric bazaars in the cities of Isfahan, Yazd and Shiraz.

My mother instilled in me a passion for Persian food, which she and her sister inherited from my grandma. They still live in Iran and while researching this book I consulted them all: their guidance made this collection of recipes possible. I hope that this book will contribute to the growing interest in Persian cuisine in the UK, and that you, the reader, will be inspired by all the things I love about Persian food.

Atoosa Sepehr

With my father at Maharloo lake in Shiraz, Iran (March 2017)

PERSIAN INGREDIENTS & TECHNIQUES

While there are traditional ways of preparing ingredients, they are often time-consuming, and younger generations of cooks have embraced technology in the kitchen to make cooking more convenient. Many of the recipes require lots of fresh herbs, and a food processor or blender saves time and effort when chopping. A food processor or blender has many other uses in the modern Persian kitchen, from chopping vegetables and nuts, to puréeing soups and sauces. I use a stand mixer with a dough hook for making bread, and in the summer I love my ice-cream machine. To finely grind dried ingredients such as rose petals and dried mint, you can use a mortar and pestle, but it's a time-consuming process so I often use a spice grinder. Saffron is easier to grind in a mortar and pestle; I add a pinch of coarse sugar to help the grinding process.

Aubergines

Aubergines can usually be used without further preparation, but some may need to be briefly soaked to remove any bitterness: if you slice the aubergine and the seeds are brown, it's a good idea to soak them. Cut the aubergines into 1cm-thick slices, half-fill a large bowl with water, add 3 tablespoons of salt and stir well. Add the aubergines (making sure all the slices are submerged) and leave for 20 minutes. Rinse and dry thoroughly with a clean tea towel.

Smoked aubergines The most authentic way to achieve a smoky flavour for aubergines is to barbecue them whole, in their skins, on an open fire or char them directly over a gas flame. Using a skewer, pierce each aubergine all the way through. Place the aubergines on the barbecue or on the flame of a gas hob on a high heat and char for about 15 minutes, turning them occasionally with metal tongs until the skin is completely burnt, flaky and blackened all over and the flesh is softened through to the centre. Set the aubergines aside to cool completely. Then, holding each aubergine by the stalk, peel off the skin (wet your fingers in a bowl of water to avoid the skin sticking to your fingers).

Alternatively, turn the oven on to its highest setting. Pierce the aubergines as above, then grill or bake for 50 minutes in the centre of the oven, turning the aubergines halfway through. Set aside to cool completely before slicing lengthways and spooning out the flesh.

Barberries

Barberries are small red berries with a sweet and sour taste, packed with vitamin C (see picture on page 68). Dried barberries are used in various Iranian dishes and you can find them in Middle Eastern shops, good supermarkets and online. They are usually rinsed before use.

Fenugreek leaves, dried

The leaves have a strong yet sweet aroma and a bitter taste, and give a unique flavour and aroma when added to a recipe. You can sometimes find fenugreek under its Indian name of *methi*.

Golden prunes

Golden prunes, or *aloo bokharah*, are similar to regular prunes but they are sweet and sour, and so sugar or honey is usually added to dishes that include golden prunes.

Golpar

Used as a spice, *golpar* is the seeds of Persian hogweed (sometimes sold as angelica seeds): you can see the seeds in the photo on page 14. *Golpar* is aromatic with a slightly bitter flavour and a lovely citrusy aroma. it can be found online or in Iranian supermarkets. The seeds are usually ground to a powder and added to pickles and some salads, or sprinkled on cooked broad beans and enjoyed as a snack.

Kashk
Kashk or Persian whey is a creamy thick liquid made from fermented sour yoghurt; it has a strong umami flavour and is used both as a flavouring and a topping for *ash* (thick soups) or dips. You can buy it from Iranian stores, Middle Eastern supermarkets or online. If you can't find it, you can blend equal quantities of sour cream and feta cheese in a food processor until they form a paste. You can also find *kashk* in dried form, which you can either reconstitute with water and use for cooking or just eat it dry as a snack.

Mint, dried
Dried mint is a really common ingredient in Iran, and is used in many dishes and toppings. Before using dried mint in a recipe, place the mint in the palm of one hand and then bring both hands together and rub the mint between your palms to finely grind the mint; the natural oils in your hand and the heat of your skin combine to bring out the scent of the mint.

Nuts
In almost every Iranian house you will see some fresh fruit and nuts on the table. Mixtures of different kinds of nuts – such as pistachios, walnuts, almonds, hazelnuts and cashews – with dried fruits and raisins are commonly served in Iranian homes. Nuts can be eaten plain, roasted with salt and lime or saffron. Nuts also play a big part in Iranian cuisine. Walnuts, pistachios and almonds are used in a wide range of dishes, both savoury and sweet. It is important to use fresh nuts, as old nuts often have a strong rancid taste, so taste them before using them.

Persian dried limes
Persian dried limes, also known as *noumi basra* or *limoo amani* or *omani lemon*, are limes that have been dried until they are rock-hard. They have a sharp flavour and are very aromatic. They can be used whole or ground to a powder and sprinkled over dishes or salads. In my recipes I have used them whole, but they need to be pierced five or six times before being used in a recipe: if you find them too hard to pierce, soak them in hot water for 5 minutes before piercing them. Before serving, to bring out the flavour of the dried lime further, press the limes against the side of the pan to release the lime juice into the dish. Then either throw the limes away or leave them in the dish. You can find dried limes online or in Iranian or Middle Eastern supermarkets. If you cannot find dried limes you could use lime juice, but you will not get the smoky, earthy flavour.

Persian rice
Persian rice looks similar to basmati rice: the uncooked grains are slightly shorter but they get longer and fluffier when they are steamed, and the aroma and flavour of Persian rice is incomparable. It's not always easy to buy Persian rice in the west, but it is not impossible. Iranian stores sometimes have rice deliveries during the year, or try online Iranian stores.

Pomegranates
The juicy, crunchy red seeds of pomegranates provide a jewel-like garnish to many Persian dishes. You can sometimes buy the seeds ready prepared, but if you have a whole pomegranate you can remove the seeds yourself. Using a sharp knife, cut a circle, at a shallow angle, 2cm around the crown of the pomegranate, and discard the crown. Cut along the ridges to mark the pomegranate into quarters, cutting just through to the red part of the pomegranate skin. Use your fingers to gently prise open the pomegranate, exposing the seeds. Hold a pomegranate quarter over a bowl, seeds-side-down, and hit the back

firmly with a wooden spoon. The seeds pop right out! Repeat with the remaining quarters.

Pomegranate molasses is pomegranate juice that has been reduced until it thickens. It varies in sourness, so taste before adding too much.

Reshteh
Reshteh is a type of Persian noodle that you can buy in Iranian or Middle Eastern supermarkets or online. If you cannot find *reshteh* then you can use udon noodles instead.

Rose water
Rose water, known as *golab* in Iran, originated in Persia, more than 1000 years ago. It is made by steeping rose petals in water then distilling the liquid. It is used in many sweets and drinks in Iran.

Saffron
Saffron is the dried threads (steams) of a type of crocus, and has been used in Iran since ancient times to add a golden colour and a distinctive flavour to both savoury and sweet recipes. If possible, use high-quality saffron, preferably Iranian, which has a deeper colour and richer flavour than many types of saffron found in the West. Iranian saffron can be found in most Iranian supermarkets or online. Saffron is usually ground first and soaked or combined with liquid before use. In my recipes I use saffron water.

Saffron water Using a pestle and mortar, grind the saffron threads together with a pinch of granulated or demerara sugar to form a fine powder. Add 2 tablespoons of boiling water and leave to infuse for at least 10 minutes. Alternatively, after grinding the saffron with sugar, sprinkle it on top of an ice cube in a small bowl and leave the ice to melt: although this is a lengthy process the flavour of saffron is preserved better.

Sumac
Sumac is a flowering shrub whose red fruits are dried and ground as a spice with a tart lemony flavour. In Iran, sumac is used commonly with various meat kebabs, as it cuts through the fat of the meat. It is used in salad dressings and sauces and is available in many supermarkets, as well as online.

Tomb of Cyrus the Great, Fars Province, Pasargadae, Iran (March 2016)

MEZZE, STARTERS & SIDES

MARINATED OLIVES WITH WALNUTS AND MINT
ZEITOON PARVARDEH

SERVES 4

60g shelled walnuts

3 tbsp pomegranate molasses

2 large garlic cloves, crushed

3 tbsp extra-virgin olive oil

2–3 tbsp fresh lime juice

10g fresh mint leaves, finely chopped

½ tbsp dried mint (see page 13)

¼ tsp freshly ground black pepper

Salt

200g good-quality pitted oil-cured green olives

Seeds from ½ pomegranate (about 150g, see page 13)

This recipe originated in northern Iran, where there are many olive groves along the Caspian Sea. *Zeitoon parvardeh* has become popular throughout Iran, served as an appetizer or as a side dish. The olives, which must be of good quality, are marinated in a tangy sauce.

Put the walnuts in a food processor and grind to a smooth paste.

In a bowl, combine the ground walnuts, pomegranate molasses, garlic, olive oil, 2 tablespoons of the lime juice, the fresh and dried mint, pepper and salt to taste (bearing in mind that the olives may be salty) and stir well. (Depending on the sourness of your pomegranate molasses you may need to add a little more lime juice.) Add the olives and pomegranate seeds and mix gently.

Chill in the fridge for at least a couple of hours before serving. Leftovers can be kept for 2 to 3 days in the fridge in a sealed glass jar.

YOGHURT WITH CUCUMBER, MINT AND DILL

MAST-O KHIAR

SERVES 4

400g baby cucumbers or 1 large cucumber

450g Greek-style or natural yoghurt

15g fresh dill leaves, finely chopped

2 tsp dried mint (see page 13)

1 garlic clove, crushed, or 40g raisins (optional)

¼ tsp freshly ground black pepper

Salt

FOR THE TOPPING

1 tbsp edible dried rose petals (optional)

1 tsp dried mint (see page 13)

30g shelled walnuts, coarsely chopped

Mast-o khiar is one of the most popular side dishes in Iran, eaten as an accompaniment to grilled meats, fried foods and many other dishes. It is cool and refreshing and I like to eat it on its own, especially in the searing heat of the Iranian summer. You can add garlic if you like, or I sometimes add raisins for a fruity flavour.

Grate the cucumber coarsely and place in a large bowl. (If you are using Greek yoghurt, add the cucumber juice, but if you are using regular yoghurt discard half of the juice as it might make the *mast-o khiar* too runny.) Add the yoghurt, dill, dried mint, garlic or raisins if using, black pepper and salt to taste and mix gently but thoroughly. (If the cucumber is very large you may want to add a couple of extra tablespoons of yoghurt.) Taste and adjust the seasoning if needed.

Sprinkle the toppings over the yoghurt and serve immediately. You can make the *mast-o khiar* up to an hour or so in advance and keep it in the fridge, but do not add the toppings until you are ready to serve.

SMOKED AUBERGINE WITH GARLIC AND YOGHURT

BORANI-E BADEMJAN

SERVES 4

3 large aubergines, smoked (see page 12)
4 tbsp olive oil
6 large garlic cloves, crushed
½ tsp ground turmeric
1½ tsp dried mint (see page 13)
Salt
¼ tsp freshly ground black pepper
300g Greek-style yoghurt (preferably full-fat)

FOR THE CRISPY FRIED ONION TOPPING

1 large onion
Vegetable oil for frying

This is a wonderfully tasty dip with a creamy texture and a deep smoky flavour. For best results, use full-fat Greek-style yoghurt. Serve as a starter with bread such as pitta or Barbary bread (page 201).

Make the crispy fried onion topping (see page 91). Set aside.

Peel the smoked aubergines (see page 12), then mash them using the back of a fork. Set aside.

Add the oil and garlic to a frying pan and cook on a low heat for a couple of minutes, stirring frequently, until the garlic is cooked and pale golden (do not rush this stage as the garlic can burn quickly). Add the turmeric and mint and stir for 20 seconds.

Add the mashed aubergines and salt to taste and mix well. Increase the heat to medium and mash the aubergines with the back of a wooden spoon.

Continue cooking and mashing for about 5 minutes or until all the liquid has evaporated and the mixture has an even consistency. Add the pepper, stir, then turn off the heat and leave to cool for 10 minutes.

Add the yoghurt and stir to mix. Taste and adjust the seasoning, then transfer the aubergine mixture to a serving dish; garnish with the crispy fried onion.

BEETROOT WITH SPINACH AND CREAMY YOGHURT

BORANI-E LABOO

SERVES 4

300g uncooked beetroot, trimmed
Olive oil for brushing
100g fresh spinach leaves
Salt
300g Greek-style yoghurt (preferably full-fat)
1 tbsp fresh lime juice
¼ tsp freshly ground black pepper
½ tbsp black or white sesame seeds to garnish

I have always loved the colour and flavour of beetroot; when combined with yoghurt it creates *borani-e laboo*, which has a wonderfully creamy texture. It is served as a side dish or as a starter. You can use ready-cooked beetroot, but be sure to use beetroot cooked in natural juice rather than in vinegar. However, by cooking the beetroot yourself you will achieve a richer and more natural taste.

Preheat the oven to 200°C/180°C fan/Gas 6. Brush the beetroot with a little olive oil and then wrap each one separately in foil and roast for 1 hour. Leave to cool completely, then peel (the skin should come off easily) and grate coarsely.

Place the spinach, a pinch of salt and 3 tablespoons of water in a saucepan, cover with a lid and cook on the lowest possible heat for 10 minutes until the spinach has wilted and turned a darker shade of green (stirring halfway through and adding a little more water if needed). Give it a good stir, turn the heat to medium and cook for 1–2 minutes or until all the water has evaporated. Set aside to cool before chopping roughly.

Place the grated beetroot, spinach, yoghurt, lime juice, pepper and a pinch of salt in a large bowl. Stir gently until they are completely mixed. Taste and add more salt if needed.

Place in the fridge for an hour; this will help blend the yoghurt and beetroot flavour and colour.

Give it a good stir and garnish with sesame seeds before serving.

GOAT'S CHEESE WITH FRESH HERBS AND WALNUTS

DOYMAJ

MAKES 25

80g shelled walnuts
10g fresh mint leaves
10g fresh tarragon leaves
5g fresh flat-leaf parsley leaves
1 spring onion
125g goat's cheese
20ml fresh lime juice
¼ tsp freshly ground black pepper
Salt (optional)
1 large cucumber, sliced into 25 discs (approx. 7mm thick)

I first came across this dish while I was a student at the University of Tabriz, a city in the north-west of Iran. *Doymaj* can be served with flat bread or pitta bread, but I really like it as a canapé, spread on small pieces of toast or on discs of cucumber. A key consideration in making this dish is the type of goat's cheese you use: you need a soft but crumbly goat's cheese rather than a creamy type.

Roughly chop the walnuts in a food processor for 5–7 seconds. Do not overchop them as they need to retain a crunchy texture. Set aside.

Add the herbs and spring onion to the food processor and blitz for 10–12 seconds or until finely chopped.

In a large bowl, finely crumble the cheese, using a fork.

Add the walnuts, herbs, lime juice and pepper to the cheese and mix well to make a paste. Taste and add salt if needed.

To serve, spoon the mixture on top of the cucumber slices.

SMOKED AUBERGINE WITH TOMATOES, GARLIC AND EGGS

MIRZA GHASEMI

SERVES 4 AS A STARTER OR 3 AS A MAIN DISH

3 large aubergines, smoked (see page 12)

600g vine tomatoes

1 large bulb of garlic, cloves separated and crushed

4 tbsp olive oil

30g good-quality tomato purée

Salt

¼ tsp ground turmeric

2 eggs

¼ tsp freshly ground black pepper

This recipe is a favourite of mine. I first came across it in northern Iran during a summer holiday with my parents. It can be served as a starter with pitta or flat bread, and I love it with Persian rice (pages 112–113) for lunch or dinner.

Peel the smoked aubergines (see page 12), then mash them using the back of a fork. Set aside.

To cook the tomatoes: if you smoked the aubergines on the barbecue, cook the tomatoes at the same time. If you used a gas flame or the oven to smoke the aubergines, then grill or bake the tomatoes in the oven at the highest setting for 25 minutes (if you smoked the aubergines in the oven, add the tomatoes at the same time and remove them when you turn the aubergines halfway through cooking). Leave to cool, then peel off the skins and roughly chop. Set aside.

Add half the garlic and half the olive oil to a saucepan and cook on a low heat, stirring frequently, until the garlic is cooked and golden at the edges (do not rush this stage as the garlic can burn quickly). Add the tomatoes (with their juice) and mash them with the back of a wooden spoon. Increase the heat to medium to high and fry for 5–7 minutes or until the juice has evaporated but the tomato sauce is not dry. Add the tomato purée and a pinch of salt, stir and fry for couple of minutes. Set aside.

Add the remaining garlic and olive oil to a large frying pan and cook on a low heat as above. Add the turmeric and stir for 30 seconds and then add the mashed aubergines (including any juice) and fry on a medium heat for 5–7 minutes until paste-like.

Add the tomato mixture to the aubergines and mix well. Taste and season if needed.

In a small bowl, lightly beat the eggs with the black pepper and a small pinch of salt.

Make several hollows in the aubergine mix and pour the beaten egg evenly over the top. Leave the pan on a medium heat for 3–5 minutes or until the egg has set. Stir gently to combine the egg with the aubergine mixture; taste and adjust the seasoning if needed before serving.

AUBERGINE AND PERSIAN KASHK DIP
KASHK-O BADEMJAN

SERVES 4 AS A STARTER OR 3 AS A MAIN DISH

3 large aubergines, peeled and sliced lengthways into 1cm-thick slices, soaked if necessary (see page 12)

3 tbsp olive oil, plus extra for brushing

Salt

2 onions, finely chopped

½ tsp ground turmeric

2–3 vine tomatoes (about 300g), finely chopped

100g *kashk* (see page 13), plus a little extra to serve

FOR THE FRIED MINT TOPPING

3 tbsp dried mint

4 tbsp olive oil

This is one of the most popular starters in Iran. The inclusion of *kashk* (see page 13), which has a strong umami flavour, combined with the soft texture of the aubergine cooked with tomatoes, gives this dish its unique taste.

The aubergines are traditionally fried in oil, but baking is a healthier option. If you can't find *kashk*, blend together 100g of sour cream and 100g of feta to make a smooth paste. *Kashk-o bademjan* is usually served with flat bread or pitta bread and is often eaten as a light lunch or dinner.

Preheat the oven to 200°C/180°C fan/Gas 6 and line two baking trays with baking parchment.

Brush the aubergines generously on both sides with olive oil and lay them on the lined baking trays in single layers. Sprinkle a pinch of salt over the top and roast for 35–40 minutes or until the edges are golden brown.

Meanwhile, add the oil and onions to a large pan on a medium heat and cook for about 15 minutes until they are soft and golden brown; stir occasionally at first and then more frequently to prevent the onions from burning. Add the turmeric and stir to mix. Set half of the onions aside to use for the topping.

Add the chopped tomatoes (with their juice) to the pan, stir, then add the aubergines. Mix well and bring to the boil, then turn the heat to the lowest setting, cover the pan with a lid and cook for 35 minutes or until the aubergines are very soft. Use the back of a wooden spoon to mash the aubergine and tomatoes to a paste. After 35 minutes all the liquid should have evaporated; if not, turn the heat to medium and stir until there is no more liquid. Add the *kashk* and mix well. Turn off the heat.

Meanwhile, make the fried mint topping (see page 91). Set aside.

Transfer the aubergine mixture into a serving dish. Top with some *kashk* and then add the fried mint topping (including the oil in which it was cooked) and the reserved onions.

CHICKEN LIVERS WITH CARAMELIZED ONION AND CORIANDER

KHORAK-E JIGAR-E MORGH

SERVES 4

4 tbsp olive oil

1 red onion, finely chopped

½ tbsp ground turmeric

400g organic chicken livers, trimmed of any sinew or tubes and cut into 3cm pieces

25g fresh coriander, finely chopped

Salt and freshly ground black pepper

This recipe, which was one of my favourite dishes when I was growing up in Iran, is packed with protein, iron and vitamin A. If possible use organic chicken livers: the natural diet of the chickens makes for healthier livers. This can be eaten as a starter or a light lunch, and it is usually served with bread and maybe a slice of lime on the side.

Add the oil and onion to a frying pan on a medium heat, stir to coat the onion in the oil, and cook for about 10 minutes, until caramelized, stirring occasionally at first and more frequently as the onion begins to change colour.

Add the turmeric and stir for 30 seconds.

Add the livers and stir well to mix with the onion. Cook for 6–8 minutes, stirring often (if you like your liver rare or well done, adjust the cooking time accordingly). Turn off the heat, add the coriander and stir to mix. Season with salt to taste and grind some black pepper on top; serve immediately.

CHEESE AND POTATO SAMOSAS
SAMBUSE SIBZAMINI

MAKES 12

150g baby new potatoes
2 tbsp olive oil
1 red onion, finely chopped
4 large garlic cloves, finely chopped
1 tbsp tomato purée
½ tsp chilli powder
1 tbsp cumin seeds
40ml fresh lime juice
50g cheddar cheese, coarsely grated
50g mozzarella cheese, coarsely grated
25g fresh coriander, finely chopped
Salt
1 ready-rolled puff pastry sheet, at room temperature
Melted butter for brushing
Sesame seeds to sprinkle

I have fond memories of my aunt making potato samosas for my brother and me when we visited her in the city of Shiraz in south-central Iran. The samosas can be eaten on their own, but I like them with chilli sauce and a small salad.

Put the potatoes in a pan, add cold water to cover and bring to the boil, then simmer until they are cooked through (do not overcook). Drain, rinse under cold water until they are completely cold, then chop into 5mm cubes.

Meanwhile, add the oil and onion to a large frying pan on a medium heat and cook for 5–7 minutes until golden brown. Add the garlic and stir for a couple of minutes. Add the tomato purée and stir well, then add the chilli powder and cumin seeds and stir for 30 seconds. (If the potatoes are not ready at this point, take the frying pan off the heat until the potatoes are ready.)

Add the chopped potatoes, stir, then add the lime juice and stir until all the juice has been absorbed. Set aside to cool completely.

Add the cheeses and coriander, stir well, taste and add salt if needed; set aside.

Preheat the oven to 200°C/180°C fan/Gas 6 and line a baking sheet with baking parchment.

Roll out the pastry sheet until it measures about 40 x 30cm and cut it into 12 squares. Place about 2 tablespoons of the filling in the centre of a square, then fold the pastry over to form a triangle and seal the edges by pressing together tightly. Place the filled pastry on the baking sheet. Repeat this process until all the pastry and filling is used up.

Brush some melted butter on top of each triangle and sprinkle over a few sesame seeds. Bake in the centre of the oven for 25–30 minutes, or until golden and crisp.

MEAT SAMOSAS

MAKES 24

2 tbsp olive oil
1 large red onion, finely chopped
2 large garlic cloves, crushed
½ tbsp cumin seeds
1 tsp ground cumin
½ tsp ground cinnamon
½ tbsp ground turmeric
Salt
400g minced lamb or beef (up to 20% fat)
½ tsp freshly ground black pepper
100g good-quality tomato purée
½–1 tsp chilli powder
50ml fresh lime juice
60g fresh coriander, finely chopped
6 sheets of filo pastry (approx. 50 x 30cm)
Melted butter for brushing
Nigella seeds to sprinkle

Although commonly associated with India, the word samosa actually derives from the Persian word *sanbosag*. Meat samosas originate from the south of Iran, where the food tends to be spicier. Traditionally, the samosas are deep-fried, but I prefer to cook them in the oven, which is a healthier option. Meat samosas can be eaten as a starter or for lunch or dinner with salad.

Add the oil and onion to a large frying pan on a medium heat and cook for about 5 minutes until the onion is soft and golden at the edges. Add the garlic and stir for a couple of minutes, then add the cumin seeds, ground cumin, cinnamon, turmeric and a pinch of salt and stir for 30 seconds. Add the meat and pepper and fry, using the back of a wooden spoon to break up the meat, until the meat is fully cooked.

Add the tomato purée and chilli powder to taste, give it a good stir and fry for a couple of minutes, then add the lime juice, stir and fry for another couple of minutes or until all the lime juice has been absorbed. Taste and adjust the seasoning, then turn off the heat and set aside to cool completely. Add the coriander and mix well.

Preheat the oven to 200°C/180°C fan/Gas 6 and line a baking sheet with baking parchment.

Unwrap the filo pastry and keep under a damp tea towel until ready to use.

Work with one sheet of filo at a time. Lay a sheet of filo on a work surface and brush with melted butter. Cut it lengthways into four strips. Take one of the pastry strips and with the shortest side facing you, spoon 1 tablespoon of the filling onto the pastry, 2cm from the bottom and 1cm in from each side of the pastry strip. Fold the bottom of the pastry over the filling and then fold in the two long sides of the pastry (all the way along the pastry strip). Roll up the pastry from the bottom, enclosing the filling, and place on the baking sheet. Repeat this process until all the pastry is used up.

Brush some melted butter over each samosa, sprinkle with nigella seeds and bake for 10–15 minutes, until golden and crisp.

Si-o-se-pol Bridge, Isfahan, Iran (March 2016)

SALADS

SHIRAZI SALAD

SERVES 4

400g baby cucumbers or 1 large cucumber

400g vine tomatoes

1 small red onion

60ml fresh lime juice

1 tbsp dried mint (see page 13)

1 tsp sumac

Salt

This is a traditional salad from Shiraz, the city where I was born and after which Shiraz wine is named. The original recipe uses sour grape juice, but it can be difficult to find in the west, so I substitute lime juice. The recipe also requires that you chop the tomatoes and cucumbers into very fine dice. If you are short of time then you can chop them into larger pieces, but don't make them too large. I do prefer to use baby cucumbers as they tend to be crunchier and less juicy.

Chop the cucumbers into cubes no bigger than 1cm. If you are using a large cucumber lay it horizontally on a chopping board. Cut long slits down the length of the cucumber from approximately 2cm from the end. Give the cucumber a half turn and cut slits the same length down the sides. Now, slice the cucumber sticks that are still attached to the end of the cucumber evenly. Place the chopped cucumber in a large bowl.

Chop the tomatoes to match the size of the cucumber and add to the bowl.

Chop the onion into similar-sized cubes and add to the bowl.

Add the lime juice, dried mint, sumac and salt to taste and stir gently to mix. Serve immediately or chill for up to half an hour before serving.

CUCUMBER, RED ONION AND POMEGRANATE SALAD

SALAD-E ANAR

SERVES 4

500g baby cucumbers or 1 large cucumber

1 red onion

Seeds from 1 pomegranate (see page 13)

1 tsp dried mint (see page 13)

5g fresh mint leaves, chopped

FOR THE DRESSING

50ml fresh lime juice

2 tsp extra-virgin olive oil

½ tsp sumac

¼ tsp *golpar* powder (optional) (see page 12)

Salt

In Iran, they call pomegranate the fruit from heaven, and as a child growing up in Isfahan, I remember taking great care not to waste a single seed. For this salad, it is best to use baby cucumbers because they tend to be crunchier. I have used *golpar* (see page 12), which has a fruity, citrusy aroma with a slight bitter edge; however, if you can't find *golpar* the salad will still be delicious.

Cut the cucumbers into slices about 3mm thick; if you are using a large cucumber, first cut it in half lengthways and slice each half separately. Add to a large bowl.

Cut the onion into fine slices to make onion rings; add to the bowl.

Add the pomegranate seeds, dried and fresh mint; set aside.

To make the dressing, place all the ingredients in a small bowl and mix well, adding salt to taste.

Add the dressing to the salad, mix well and serve immediately.

CARAMELIZED ONION AND CHICKPEA SALAD
SALAD-E NOKHOD

SERVES 4

2 x 400g tins of chickpeas, rinsed and drained

Salt

4 large red onions, cut in half and then finely sliced into half-moon shapes

7 tbsp olive oil

3 large garlic cloves, crushed

2 tsp ground cumin

1 tsp cumin seeds

40ml fresh lime juice

2 tsp sumac

20g fresh chives, finely chopped

30g fresh coriander, finely chopped

160g feta cheese, crumbled

This delicious salad, fragrant with garlic and cumin, can be eaten on its own or as a side to a main dish. As with all my recipes, I strongly recommend using dried beans and chickpeas. However, if you are too busy to go through the process of soaking and cooking dried chickpeas (see note), I have used tinned chickpeas to make this recipe less time consuming.

Put the chickpeas, 500ml water and 1 teaspoon of salt in a saucepan, bring to the boil and then simmer on a low heat for 10 minutes. Drain and set aside.

Meanwhile, add the onions and olive oil to a frying pan on a medium heat and stir to coat the onions in the oil. Cook for about 15 minutes until caramelized, stirring occasionally at first and more frequently as the onions begin to change colour.

Add the garlic and stir for a minute. Add the ground cumin and cumin seeds and stir for 30 seconds and then add the chickpeas and mix well. Transfer to a large bowl.

Add the lime juice, sumac, chives, coriander and feta cheese to the bowl and mix well. Season with salt to taste and serve immediately.

Note
If you prefer to use dried chickpeas, soak 200g of dried chickpeas in water for 48 hours, changing the water every 12 hours (the longer you soak the chickpeas the less time they will take to cook). Rinse the soaked chickpeas, place in a pan with 1.5 litres of water and 1 tablespoon of salt and bring to the boil. Using a large spoon, skim off the foam on the surface of the water; turn the heat to the lowest setting, cover with a lid and simmer for 2½–3 hours, or for 1 hour in a pressure cooker. If the chickpeas have been sitting in a cupboard for a long time they will take longer to cook; better to use newly bought chickpeas.

SALAD OLIVIEH

SERVES 6-8

400g baby new potatoes

Salt

200g carrots, peeled

2 roasted chicken breasts or ½ a roasted chicken

4 eggs, hard-boiled, chopped into 1cm cubes

100g tinned sweetcorn, drained

100g petits pois (fresh or frozen), boiled for 2 minutes, drained

200g pickled cucumbers/cornichons (ideally in brine), chopped into 1cm cubes

2 celery sticks, chopped into 5mm cubes

20g fresh flat-leaf parsley, finely chopped

FOR THE DRESSING

300g mayonnaise

100g Greek-style yoghurt

60ml fresh lime juice

¼ tsp freshly ground black pepper

1 tsp Dijon mustard (optional)

This is the most commonly served salad in Iran, although it has its origins in Russia. It combines potatoes, vegetables, eggs, meat and mayonnaise and is often added to picnic baskets and served as a sandwich filling in a fresh baguette. It can also be eaten on its own or as canapés.

Put the potatoes in a pan, add ½ teaspoon of salt and cold water to cover and bring to the boil, then simmer until they are cooked through (do not overcook). Drain, rinse under cold water until they are completely cold, then chop into 1cm cubes and set aside.

Cook the carrots in boiling water until just tender, rinse under cold water and chop into 1cm cubes. Set aside.

Shred the chicken meat, discarding the skin and bones, and add to a large bowl, together with the potato and carrot cubes. Add all the remaining salad ingredients (ensure they are cold before you add the dressing).

In a separate bowl, mix all the dressing ingredients together, adding salt to taste.

Add the dressing to the salad bowl and mix well. Taste and adjust the salt, pepper and lime juice if needed. Chill in the fridge for a couple of hours for the flavours to blend before serving.

Tip
Instead of roasted chicken, you can use poached chicken: cut two chicken breast fillets into approximately 3cm pieces and put in a pan with 150ml water, 1 peeled and quartered onion, 1 tsp ground turmeric, ¼ tsp ground black pepper and a good pinch of salt. Bring to the boil and then cover and simmer on the lowest setting for 25 minutes or until the chicken is cooked through. Leave until cold before shredding and adding to the salad.

PERSIAN POTATO SALAD
SALAD-E SIBZAMINI

SERVES 4

1kg baby new potatoes

Salt

8 eggs, hard-boiled and peeled

20g fresh dill leaves, finely chopped

20g fresh chives, finely chopped

120g pickled cucumbers/cornichons (ideally in brine), chopped into 1cm cubes

4 celery sticks, finely chopped

2 tbsp pumpkin seeds

FOR THE DRESSING

100g plain yoghurt

100g mayonnaise

1½ tsp Dijon mustard

40ml fresh lime juice

¼ tsp freshly ground black pepper

My grandma used to make this salad for me when I was a child: whenever I eat it, I think of her and the care and affection she put into preparing this recipe. It is easy to make and is a great addition to a picnic basket.

Put the potatoes in a pan, add 1 teaspoon of salt and cold water to cover and bring to the boil, then simmer until they are cooked through (do not overcook). Drain, rinse under cold water until they are completely cold, then chop into 2cm pieces and set aside.

Cut each egg lengthways into four wedges and set aside.

To make the dressing, place all the ingredients in a small bowl and mix well until rich and creamy, adding salt to taste.

Put the potatoes into a large bowl, add the dill, chives, cornichons and celery and the dressing and mix well. Finally, add the egg wedges and mix gently so the eggs don't break up. Chill in the fridge for a couple of hours before serving, garnished with pumpkin seeds.

WATERMELON, FETA CHEESE AND MINT SALAD

SALAD-E HENDAVANEH

SERVES 4

1.5kg watermelon flesh

200–250g feta cheese

Seeds from 1 pomegranate (see page 13)

40g shelled walnuts, roughly chopped

15g shelled pistachios, roughly chopped

20g fresh mint leaves, roughly chopped

1 tbsp nigella seeds

This cool and juicy watermelon salad is perfect on a hot summer's day. For best results use a ripe, sweet and crunchy watermelon and chill in the fridge before preparing it. In Iran the combination of flat bread, cheese and watermelon is quite common; if you like, serve toasted flat bread alongside your salad.

Cut the watermelon into cubes (approximately 2cm) and deseed.

Cut the feta cheese into cubes (approximately 1cm).

Combine all the ingredients in a large bowl and gently mix before serving.

CHARGRILLED AUBERGINE AND BEETROOT WITH SAFFRON YOGHURT
SALAD-E LABOO

SERVES 4

500g uncooked beetroot, trimmed
Vegetable oil for brushing
3 large garlic cloves, crushed
150ml extra-virgin olive oil
3 large aubergines, sliced into 1cm-thick discs
Salt
300g brown mushrooms, thinly sliced
100g feta cheese, crumbled
15g fresh flat-leaf parsley, chopped
Seeds from ½ pomegranate (about 150g, see page 13)
Freshly ground black pepper

FOR THE SAFFRON YOGHURT DRESSING

1–2 generous pinches of saffron threads
Pinch of granulated or demerara sugar
140g Greek-style yoghurt
20ml fresh lime juice
1 tsp clear honey
Pinch of chilli powder
Pinch of salt

This salad combines the sweetness of beetroot and pomegranate with the saltiness of feta cheese and the smoky flavour of grilled aubergine and mushrooms, topped with saffron yoghurt. When I make this salad, I remember my mother sending me out to buy freshly cooked beetroot on the streets of Isfahan, where it is sold from large trolleys.

First, make the saffron water (see page 15) and set aside.

Preheat the oven to 200°C/180°C fan/Gas 6. Brush the beetroot with a little vegetable oil and then wrap each one separately in foil and roast for 1 hour. Leave to cool, then peel (the skin should come off easily) and cut into roughly 2–4cm pieces. Set aside.

Meanwhile, in a small bowl, mix the garlic and extra-virgin olive oil. Heat a griddle pan on a medium heat and, as soon as it is hot, brush it lightly with vegetable oil. Brush one side of the aubergine discs with the garlic oil and sprinkle some salt on top. Chargrill for 5–8 minutes, then brush the tops with garlic oil, turn over and grill for a further 5–8 minutes (the aubergines should be quite soft on the inside and crispy on the outside with brown griddle marks). Set aside.

Put the mushrooms and the remaining garlic oil in a large bowl and mix well, adding more oil if needed. Chargrill the mushrooms on the griddle pan for 3–4 minutes, stirring to ensure they are evenly cooked. Set aside.

To make the dressing, combine the yoghurt with the lime juice, honey, chilli and salt in a small bowl. Add the saffron water and mix well. Set aside.

Arrange the aubergine slices on a serving dish with the mushrooms and beetroot. Add the feta cheese and then drizzle over the saffron yoghurt dressing; finally, scatter over the chopped parsley and pomegranate seeds, season with black pepper and serve.

CARAMELIZED NUTS IN LEAF CUPS
SALAD-E CHAHAR MAGHZ

MAKES 15 CUPS
40g shelled walnuts
40g shelled hazelnuts
40g shelled pistachios
40g shelled almonds
2 tbsp sesame seeds
2 tbsp honey
15 baby gem lettuce leaves

FOR THE DRESSING
1 tsp wholegrain mustard
2 tbsp apple cider vinegar
1½ tbsp olive oil
Small pinch of salt

Although not an authentic Iranian recipe, this is inspired by Iranian cuisine. It is extremely popular among my friends and family and it has become one of my mother's favourite things to eat. It can be served as a starter or as canapés.

Break the walnuts into roughly 1cm pieces.

Put the walnuts, hazelnuts, pistachios, almonds and sesame seeds into a large frying pan on a medium heat, stirring frequently, for 3–5 minutes or until the sesame seeds are golden.

Add the honey and stir frequently for 2–3 minutes or until caramelized.

Spoon the caramelized nuts onto a large plate in a single layer and set aside to cool completely. (If you are making the caramelized nuts in advance (no more than 24 hours), cover the plate with cling film and store in the fridge to prevent them from becoming sticky.)

Stir all the dressing ingredients together in a small bowl and set aside.

Arrange the lettuce leaves on a serving platter and place the caramelized nuts onto the leaves (the nuts are likely to stick together so make sure you break them apart). Sprinkle some dressing on top of each leaf cup and serve.

"I caught the happy virus last night
When I was out singing beneath the stars.
It is remarkably contagious –

So kiss me."

Hafez

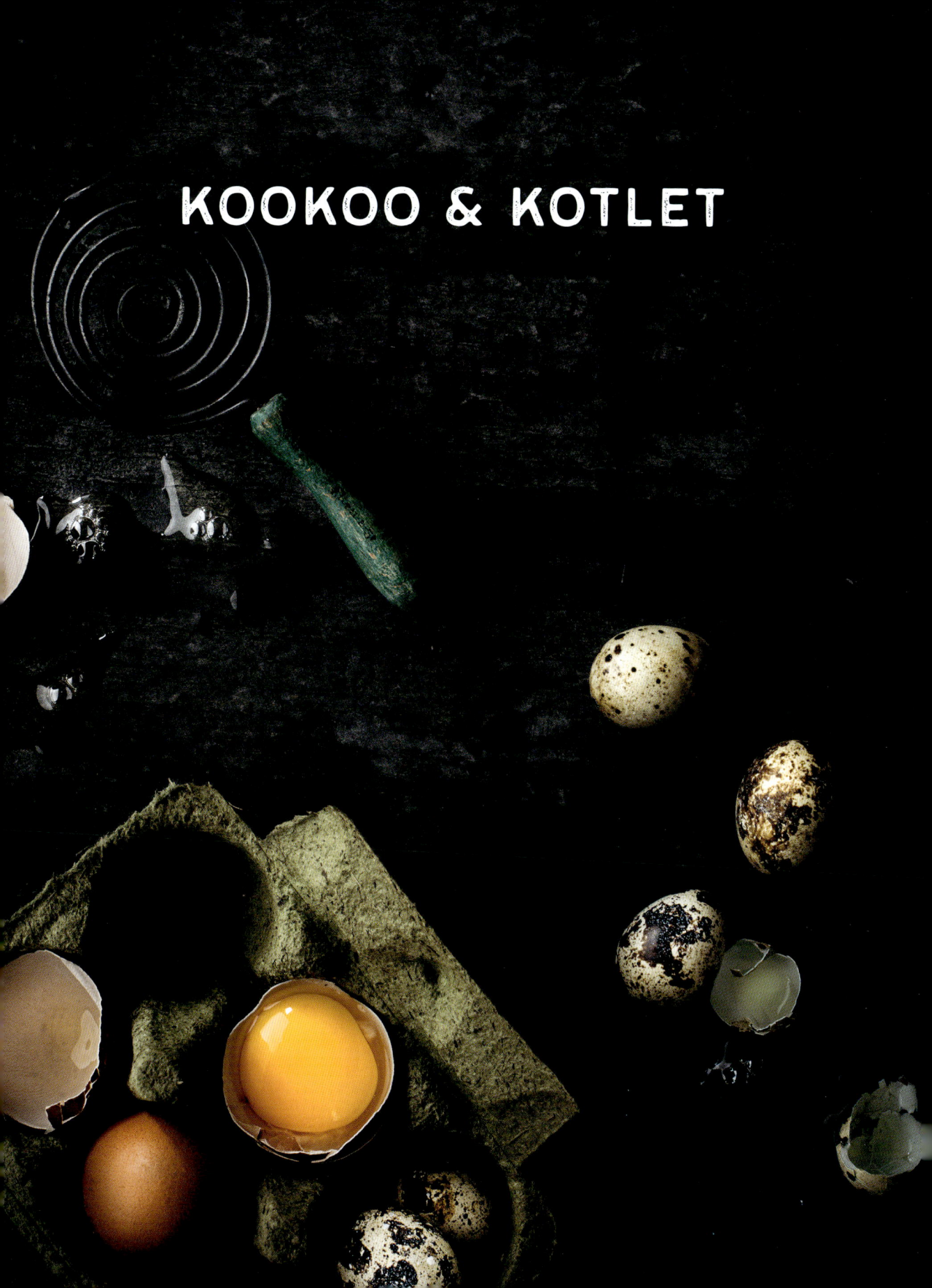

KOOKOO & KOTLET

SALMON, BROAD BEAN AND DILL FRITTATA

KOOKOO MAHI

SERVES 4

350g podded broad beans (fresh or frozen)

1½ tsp salt

4 tbsp vegetable oil

2 large skinless fillets of salmon (about 400g)

5 eggs

1 tsp ground turmeric

1 tsp ground cumin

¼ tsp freshly ground black pepper

30ml fresh lime juice

5 spring onions, finely sliced

2 large garlic cloves, crushed

25g fresh dill leaves, finely chopped

Kookoo is an egg-based dish that is similar to the Italian frittata. This version with fish originates from northern Iran; it can be served as a main dish or as a starter and is usually served with flat bread (or you can serve your favourite bread), a selection of pickles and/or salad.

Place the broad beans in a pan, add ½ teaspoon of salt and 500ml of boiling water, bring to the boil and simmer for 3–6 minutes or until the beans float in the water and are tender (cooking time will depend on the size and tenderness of the beans). Drain in a colander and rinse under cold running water to prevent the beans from cooking further. Squeeze the beans out of their skins, split the large beans in two and set aside.

Heat 1 tablespoon of oil in a frying pan and fry the salmon on a medium heat for about 2–5 minutes on each side, until golden. Transfer to a plate to cool before breaking into small flakes with a fork.

In a large bowl, lightly beat the eggs and mix in the turmeric, cumin, black pepper, lime juice and the remaining salt. Add the broad beans, flaked salmon, spring onions, garlic and dill, and mix well.

Add the remaining oil to a large non-stick frying pan (about 30cm in diameter), pour in the mixture and level the surface with a spoon. Cook on a low heat for 20–25 minutes or until the edges are firm and slightly golden.

Place the pan under a hot grill for 5–10 minutes or until the surface of the *kookoo* is golden. Cut into wedges and transfer to a serving dish.

Tip
If you do not have a large non-stick frying pan, you can cover the base of your pan with baking parchment before adding the oil.

BROAD BEANS WITH GARLIC, DILL AND EGG

BAGHALI GHATOGH

SERVES 4

750g podded broad beans (fresh or frozen)

Salt

3 tbsp olive oil

2 large onions, finely chopped

6 large garlic cloves, finely chopped

2 tsp ground turmeric

50g butter

30g fresh dill leaves, finely chopped

Freshly ground black pepper

4 eggs

This delicious dish is from the Gilan province in northern Iran. Like so many recipes from the north of the country, it includes a generous amount of garlic. The combination of cooked garlic, butter, turmeric and dill produces a beautiful aroma and taste. I like to use baby broad beans even though they take longer to prepare. *Baghali ghatogh* can be eaten with bread or with rice and served for lunch or dinner.

Place the broad beans in a pan, add 1 teaspoon of salt and 1 litre of boiling water, bring to the boil and simmer for 3–6 minutes or until the beans float and are tender (cooking time will depend on the size and tenderness of the beans). Drain in a colander and rinse under cold running water to prevent the beans from cooking further. Squeeze the beans out of their skins and set aside.

Add the oil and onions to a large frying pan (about 30cm in diameter, ideally non-stick), put on a low to medium heat, stir to coat the onion in the oil, and fry for 10 minutes or until soft and lightly golden, stirring occasionally at first and then more frequently to prevent the onions from burning.

Add the garlic and cook for a further 2 minutes, then add the turmeric and stir for 20 seconds before adding the butter, stir until the butter has melted and then add the broad beans and chopped dill. Mix well and season to taste. Cook for a couple of minutes, stirring constantly.

Break the eggs onto the bean mixture in four different places and give the pan a couple of shakes to spread the egg white. Cook, uncovered, for 12–15 minutes or until the egg whites have turned opaque. (If after 8–10 minutes the beans look dry or likely to burn, put the lid on for 2–3 minutes until the eggs are cooked to your liking.) Sprinkle some freshly ground black pepper on top before serving.

FRESH HERB FRITTATA WITH FETA CHEESE

KOOKOO SABZI

SERVES 4

70g fresh coriander

50g fresh flat-leaf parsley

25g fresh dill leaves

60g fresh spinach leaves

50g cos lettuce, finely shredded

70g spring onions, finely sliced

1 red onion, coarsely grated

70g shelled walnuts, coarsely chopped

25g dried barberries, rinsed (see page 12)

6 eggs

½ tsp ground turmeric

1 tsp ground cumin

¼ tsp freshly ground black pepper

½ tsp salt

3 tbsp vegetable oil

100g feta cheese, chopped into 1cm cubes

This dish is popular throughout Iran, especially for Persian New Year, around 21 March. The colour green represents rebirth and the eggs represent fertility; this recipe is a nod to the bounty of the coming spring. The traditional recipe does not include feta cheese but I like to add it to enhance the flavour. The frittata can be eaten hot or cold, as a starter or a light dinner or lunch. It is usually eaten with bread, pickles, tomatoes and olives.

Finely chop the herbs and spinach, ideally in a food processor. In a large bowl, add all the chopped herbs, lettuce, spring onions, grated onion, walnuts and barberries, eggs, turmeric, cumin, black pepper and salt. Stir well until fully mixed.

Pour the oil into a large non-stick frying pan (about 30cm in diameter) on a low heat. Immediately add the egg mixture and level the surface with a spoon. It is best not to heat the oil before adding the mixture because the base of the *kookoo* will cook too quickly and burn before the middle is cooked.

Sprinkle the feta cubes evenly on top and press them down gently so they are not sitting proud in the mixture. Cook for 20–25 minutes, keeping the heat low, until the edges are firm and slightly golden.

Place the pan under a hot grill for 5–10 minutes or until the surface of the *kookoo* is slightly golden. Cut into wedges and transfer to a serving dish.

Tip
If you do not have a large non-stick frying pan, you can cover the base of your pan with baking parchment before adding the oil.

PERSIAN OMELETTE
OMLET-E GOJEH FARANGI

SERVES 4

50g butter

1 tbsp olive oil

2 large red onions, cut in half and then finely sliced into half-moon shapes

5 large garlic cloves, finely chopped

½ tbsp cumin seeds

200g mushrooms, finely sliced

650g vine tomatoes, finely chopped

50g good-quality tomato purée

½ tsp freshly ground black pepper

Up to ¼ tsp chilli powder

Salt

20g fresh coriander, finely chopped, plus extra to garnish

4 eggs

This Iranian egg dish is usually eaten at breakfast time but it is also popular for lunch or dinner. I was always excited when my mother made this for breakfast and I could smell the aroma of fried onions and garlic from my bed. I like to add a little extra chilli and I usually serve this with bread.

Melt the butter in a large frying pan (about 30cm in diameter, ideally non-stick), on a medium heat. Add the oil and onions and stir well to coat the onions in the butter. Fry for about 12 minutes, until completely soft and beginning to turn golden brown, stirring occasionally at first and more frequently as the onions begin to change colour. Add the garlic and fry for 2 minutes, stirring constantly.

Add the cumin and give it a good stir, then add the mushrooms, mix well and cook for 3 minutes, stirring constantly.

Add the chopped tomatoes, tomato purée, pepper, chilli and salt to taste and stir well. Bring to the boil. Place a lid on the pan and simmer for 15 minutes on a low to medium heat until the tomatoes are completely cooked, giving it a good stir halfway through. Add the coriander, stir, then taste and adjust the seasoning.

Break the eggs onto the tomato mixture in four different places and cook, uncovered, for 15 minutes or until the egg whites have turned opaque. (If after 10–12 minutes the tomato mixture looks dry, put the lid on for 2–3 minutes until the eggs are cooked to your liking.)

Sprinkle some freshly ground black pepper and chopped coriander over the dish before serving.

PERSIAN POTATO PATTIES
KOOKOO SIBZAMINI

MAKES 20

600g small to medium potatoes

Salt

30g fresh chives

5 eggs

½ tbsp ground turmeric

1 tsp ground cumin

¼ tsp freshly ground black pepper

1 onion, coarsely grated

50g shelled walnuts, coarsely chopped

15g dried barberries, rinsed (see page 12)

Vegetable oil for frying

When I was a child, my mother often made *kookoo sibzamini* and I used to complain because I thought that these potato patties were quite boring. However, I grew to love them and they are now one of my favourite Iranian dishes. They are easy to make, requiring three basic ingredients – eggs, potatoes and turmeric. They can be served warm or cold and are suitable for a light lunch or dinner. They are also a nice addition to a picnic basket.

Put the potatoes in a pan, add ½ tablespoon of salt and cold water to cover, bring to the boil and boil until tender. Drain and rinse under cold running water, then set aside to cool before peeling off the skins. Grate the potatoes coarsely and place in a large bowl.

Gather the bunch of chives together, line them up and chop into 1cm pieces. Add the chives to the bowl of potatoes, then add the eggs, turmeric, cumin, black pepper, ½ teaspoon of salt, the onion, walnuts and barberries. Stir thoroughly.

Heat 5–6 tablespoons of oil in a large non-stick frying pan on a medium heat. When the oil is very hot, place a large tablespoon of the potato mixture into the pan and flatten it gently to make a patty. Make a few more patties in the same way, but do not place too many patties in the pan as this will make it difficult to turn them over.

Cook the patties for about 3–4 minutes or until golden brown underneath. Using a spatula, turn the patties over and cook for a further 2–3 minutes; add more oil to the pan if needed. Drain on a plate lined with kitchen paper to absorb excess fat while you cook the remaining patties. Serve warm or cold.

MINCED MEAT AND POTATO CAKES
KOTLET

MAKES 14

400g small to medium potatoes
1½ tsp salt
60g dried breadcrumbs
300g minced lamb (up to 20% fat)
1 small onion, coarsely grated
1 tsp ground turmeric
½ tsp freshly ground black pepper
1 tsp ground cumin
½ tsp ground cinnamon
1 tsp paprika
1 tbsp plain flour
25g fresh coriander, finely chopped
1 egg
Vegetable oil for frying

Kotlet is very popular in Iran: crunchy outside, moist in the middle, the patties can be eaten on their own or with flat bread and salad or between bread buns with some lettuce, tomato slices, pickled cucumbers/cornichons and red onion. When my mom cooked them for us, she had to hide them from me and my brother, otherwise half of the patties were gone before they got to the table. *Kotlet* can be served warm or cold, and they are great for parties and picnics.

Put the potatoes in a pan, add 1 teaspoon of salt and cold water to cover, bring to the boil, then boil until tender. Drain and rinse under cold running water, peel off the skins, then grate coarsely. Set aside to cool completely.

Put the breadcrumbs in a food processor and grind to a powder, then transfer to a large flat plate and set aside.

In a large bowl, combine the cold grated potatoes, minced meat, onion, turmeric, black pepper, cumin, cinnamon, paprika, flour, coriander, egg and the remaining salt. Using your hand, knead together for about 4 minutes or until all the ingredients are evenly mixed.

Wet your hands and take a piece of the meat mixture approximately the size of a golf ball; shape it into a ball, then flatten it on the plate of breadcrumbs (approximately 1cm thick). Flip it over to ensure that breadcrumbs cover both sides. Place the patty on a large tray and then repeat this process until all the meat mixture is used up (the patties should form a single layer on the tray).

Heat 5–6 tablespoons of oil in a large non-stick frying pan on a low to medium heat. Add some patties to the pan (do not overcrowd the pan) and fry for about 7 minutes or until a crisp crust forms on the edge. Using a spatula, carefully flip the patties over and cook until the other side is golden brown (do not flip too soon otherwise the patties may break up). Add more oil to the pan if needed.

Drain on a plate lined with kitchen paper to absorb excess fat while you fry the remaining patties.

Young Iranian Woman, Isfahan, Iran (April 2017)

SOUPS

TOPPINGS FOR ASH

Ash is like soup but is usually thicker and contains grains, beans and fresh herbs. It has been central to Persian cuisine since ancient times and today it is one of the most popular dishes in Iran. In fact, chefs in Iran are commonly referred to as *ashpaz*, which translates as 'the person who makes *ash*'. Because *ash* can be quite filling, people often have it as a meal in itself, with a piece of bread. Many takeaway shops in Iran just sell different kinds of *ash*, either in small bowls to eat as a snack or in bigger containers to take home to serve.

An important part of *ash* is the topping, and I describe three common toppings below:

Crispy fried onion: this is called *piaz dagh* in Iran, and is a popular topping not just for *ash*, but also for a wide range of dishes. Cut the onions in half and then slice finely into half-moon shapes (try to slice them all the same size). Add 300–400ml of vegetable oil, depending on the number of onions, to a medium saucepan (about 18cm in diameter) and place on a medium heat until piping hot. Add the onions in batches (if the recipe requires two onions, fry them in two or three batches), give them a good stir, and fry for 7–10 minutes or until almost golden brown, stirring occasionally; keep in mind that onions can burn quite quickly. Using a slotted spoon, remove the onions from the oil and drain in a single layer on a tray lined with kitchen paper.

Crispy fried garlic: this is known as *sir dagh* in Iran. Chop the garlic into small cubes or fine slices. Add a good glug of vegetable oil to a saucepan and place on a medium heat until piping hot. Add the garlic and stir frequently for a couple of minutes until the garlic is golden (take care not to burn the garlic as this will result in a bitter taste). Using a slotted spoon, remove the garlic from the oil and drain on a plate lined with kitchen paper. Note that if you make the crispy fried onion topping first, you can use the same oil to fry the garlic.

Fried mint: this is known as *naana dagh* in Iran and is commonly used as a topping for different kinds of *ash* and dips. Take 3 tablespoons of dried mint and, in small batches, place on the palm of one hand then bring both hands together and rub the mint between your palms to finely grind the mint; the natural oils in your hand and the heat of your skin combine to bring out the scent of the mint. Set aside. Heat 4 tablespoons of olive oil in a small saucepan and as soon as the oil is piping hot, add the dried mint, then remove the pan from the heat to allow the mint to fry slowly in the oil.

TURNIP SOUP WITH MEATBALLS
ASH-E SHALGHAM

SERVES 6
60g fresh coriander
40g fresh flat-leaf parsley
50g fresh dill leaves
80g fresh chives
80g fresh spinach leaves
5 tbsp olive oil
3 large onions, finely chopped
6 large garlic cloves, finely chopped
2 tbsp ground turmeric
1 tbsp ground cumin
¼ tsp freshly ground black pepper, plus extra to serve
80g basmati rice, rinsed
100g whole mung beans
2.2 litres good-quality beef stock
2 turnips (about 600g), peeled and cut into 3cm cubes

FOR THE MEATBALLS
300g minced lamb or beef (up to 20% fat)
1 small onion, coarsely grated
1 tsp ground turmeric
½ tsp ground cumin
½ tsp ground cinnamon
Pinch of chilli powder
¼ tsp freshly ground black pepper
½ tsp salt

FOR THE TOPPING (optional) (see page 91)
2 onions for crispy fried onion
Vegetable oil for frying

My mother used to make this soup for me and my brother during the winter time, especially if one of us was suffering from a cold. Turnips in Iran tend to be sweeter than those found in many western countries, so if I can't find good turnips I sometimes use swede instead. To make a vegetarian version of this soup, omit the meatballs and add one more turnip to the recipe and use vegetable stock.

Finely chop the herbs and spinach, ideally in a food processor, and set aside.

In a large heavy-based pan, add the olive oil and the onions, stir to mix, and cook on a medium heat for 20 minutes or until the onions are soft and golden brown (do not rush this stage as the cooked onions form the base of the soup). Stir occasionally at first and more frequently as the onions begin to change colour to prevent them from burning.

Add the garlic and stir for 3 minutes. Add the turmeric, cumin and pepper, mix well and then add the rice and mung beans and give it a good stir. Add the stock and bring to the boil. Turn the heat to the lowest setting, put the lid on and simmer for about 30 minutes.

While the rice is cooking, make the meatballs: add all the ingredients to a large bowl and knead with your hand until evenly mixed, then shape into small meatballs (about 2–3cm in diameter). Set aside.

Make the crispy fried onion topping, if using.

Add the turnips and chopped herbs to the soup pan, mix well and bring to the boil. Add the meatballs and bring back to the boil, then turn the heat to the lowest setting, put the lid on and simmer for 35 minutes or until the turnips are tender. Taste and adjust the seasoning if needed, and cook for a couple of minutes on a medium heat without the lid.

To serve, ladle into bowls and sprinkle some freshly ground black pepper on top, then add some crispy fried onion if you like.

PERSIAN PEARL BARLEY SOUP
SOUP-E JO

SERVES 6

2 skinless chicken thighs on the bone, all the fat removed

1 large onion, peeled

200g pearl barley, rinsed

2 litres chicken stock

1 tsp ground turmeric

½ tsp ground white pepper

1 carrot (about 120–150g), coarsely grated

200g button mushrooms, finely sliced

2 tbsp plain flour

20g butter, at room temperature

250ml milk

150ml single cream

60ml fresh lime juice

Salt

30g fresh flat-leaf parsley, chopped, to garnish

This is one of the most popular soups in Iran and when I eat it my mind always wanders back to when I was a young teenager in Iran and my parents would take me and my brother to a local restaurant as a special treat; I would always order barley soup as a starter. This is a rich and creamy soup that is perfect for a cold winter's day.

Put the chicken into a large heavy-based pan, add the onion, barley, chicken stock, turmeric and pepper. Give it a good stir and bring to the boil, then turn the heat to the lowest setting, put the lid on and simmer for 45 minutes.

Remove the onion and chicken from the stock, discard the onion and leave the chicken to cool a little before shredding it and putting it back in the pan (discard the bones).

Add the carrot and mushrooms and bring back to the boil, then turn the heat to the lowest setting, put the lid on and simmer for 10 minutes or until the carrot is cooked.

Meanwhile, make a béchamel sauce: put the flour in a saucepan and cook on a low heat for 3 minutes, stirring constantly. Remove the pan from the heat, add the butter and mix until smooth. Gradually add the milk, stirring with a balloon whisk until the flour paste has completely dissolved (if the sauce is lumpy, press it through a fine-mesh sieve two or three times until smooth). Place the pan on a medium heat and stir continuously for a couple of minutes, then add the cream and stir until it begins to boil. Gradually stir the béchamel into the pan of soup, put the lid on and cook for a further 10 minutes.

Add the lime juice and season with salt to taste. Cook for 3–5 minutes on a medium heat without the lid.

To serve, ladle into bowls and garnish generously with chopped parsley.

YOGHURT AND CHICKPEA SOUP
ASH-E DOOGH

SERVES 6

1kg full-fat yoghurt

1 egg

1 tbsp plain flour

Salt

150g Grana Padano cheese, finely grated

400g tin of chickpeas, drained and rinsed

250g baby spinach, roughly chopped

120g *reshteh* (see page 15) or udon noodle, broken into three equal pieces

60g fresh chives

60g fresh coriander

4 large garlic cloves, crushed

FOR THE TOPPING

(see page 91)

3 tbsp dried mint for fried mint

Olive oil for frying

I first tasted this yoghurt and chickpea soup in Ardabil, an ancient city in Iranian Azerbaijan. On my first visit to Ardabil I was surprised to hear Iranians speaking Azari rather than Farsi. One year later I went to study in the city of Tabriz, which, like Ardabil, is in the region of Azerbaijan. Living in Tabriz gave me the opportunity to learn the Azari language and culture. Iranians use sour yoghurt in this recipe, but as this can be difficult to find in western countries, I have combined Grana Padano cheese with plain yoghurt to create a similar taste.

In a large heavy-based pan, combine the yoghurt, egg, flour and 1 teaspoon of salt, stir until smooth and then add 1.5 litres of cold water. Using a balloon whisk, stir until the yoghurt mixture and water are completely mixed. When there are no lumps, place the pan on a high heat. Whisk constantly until the mixture comes to the boil (it is important to stir this from the moment you place it on the heat until it comes to boiling point to prevent the yoghurt from curdling). Add the cheese and whisk until the cheese has fully melted into the yoghurt mixture.

Add the chickpeas, spinach and *reshteh* and stir with a large spoon for a couple of minutes to ensure that the noodles do not stick together. Bring back to the boil and then simmer on a low heat for 15 minutes, stirring occasionally.

Meanwhile, make the fried mint topping. Set aside.

Gather the bunch of chives together, line them up and chop into 1cm pieces. Finely chop the coriander, ideally in a food processor. Add the chopped chives, coriander and garlic to the yoghurt mixture and stir for a couple of minutes.

To serve, ladle into bowls and spoon on some of the fried mint topping (including the oil in which it was cooked). Mix well before eating.

HOT BEAN SOUP
LUBIA GARM

SERVES 6

9 tbsp olive oil

5 large onions, cut in half and then finely sliced into half-moon shapes

1½ tbsp ground turmeric

300g pinto beans, soaked overnight, drained

150g white beans, soaked overnight, drained

½ tsp freshly ground black pepper

1.5 litres beef or bone stock

600g mushrooms, finely sliced

100g good-quality tomato purée

¼–1 tsp chilli powder

Salt

Extra-virgin olive oil and fresh lime juice to serve (optional)

This bean soup is packed with protein. It is one of those dishes that you will often see in parties alongside other snacks. If possible, use a good-quality beef stock; I like to make my own beef stock or bone broth but you could use vegetable stock if you want to serve this as a vegetarian dish. This soup should be quite spicy, but add chilli powder to your taste.

In a large heavy-based pan, add 5 tablespoons of the olive oil and the onions and cook on a medium heat for 20–25 minutes or until the onions are soft and golden brown (do not rush this stage as the cooked onions form the base of the soup). Stir occasionally at first and more frequently as the onions begin to change colour to prevent them from burning.

Add the turmeric and stir well for 1 minute before adding the beans, black pepper and beef stock. Mix well and bring to the boil and then turn the heat to the lowest setting, put the lid on and simmer for 1½ hours.

Meanwhile, in a large frying pan, cook the mushrooms with the remaining olive oil on a medium heat for 5 minutes or until the mushrooms are soft and juicy. Set aside.

Add the cooked mushrooms (including their juice) to the bean soup and stir well. Bring back to the boil and then turn the heat to the lowest setting, put the lid on and simmer for a further 40 minutes or until the beans are fully cooked.

Add the tomato purée and chilli powder to taste and stir well. Taste and adjust the seasoning if needed. Cook for 3 minutes on a medium heat without the lid. The soup should be thick: if it is too runny then boil further until it thickens; if it is too thick, add some boiling water or stock and boil for a minute or two.

Ladle into bowls and add a swirl of olive oil, mixed with lime juice if you like, to each bowl.

PERSIAN NOODLE AND HERB SOUP
ASH-E RESHTEH

SERVES 6

100g green lentils, rinsed
50g fresh coriander
50g fresh flat-leaf parsley leaves
50g fresh dill leaves
40g fresh mint leaves
30g fresh chives
100g fresh spinach leaves
80g spring onions
3 tbsp olive oil
2 large red onions, finely chopped
5 large garlic cloves, finely chopped
1 tsp ground turmeric
¼ tsp freshly ground black pepper
60g chickpeas, soaked overnight, drained
60g pinto beans, soaked overnight, drained
2.25 litres vegetable stock
150g *reshteh* (see page 15) or udon noodle, broken into three equal pieces
Salt
150g *kashk* (see page 13), plus extra for topping (or blend 150g sour cream with 150g feta cheese to a paste in a food processor)

FOR THE TOPPINGS
(see page 91)
3 onions for crispy fried onion
6 large garlic cloves for crispy fried garlic
3 tbsp dried mint for fried mint
Vegetable and olive oil for frying

Ash-e reshteh is a thick soup traditionally cooked for Persian New Year and the noodles symbolize good fortune. However, these days it is hugely popular in Iran and is eaten all year round.

Soak the lentils in a bowl of water and set aside.

Finely chop all the herbs, spinach and spring onions, ideally in a food processor, and set aside.

Add the oil and onions to a large heavy-based pan and fry on a medium heat for 12 minutes or until the onions are soft and golden brown. Add the garlic and stir for 3 minutes. Add the turmeric and pepper and stir for 30 seconds.

Add the drained chickpeas, pinto beans and stock to the onions and bring to the boil. Turn the heat to the lowest setting, put the lid on and simmer for 2¼ hours.

Drain the lentils and add to the pan along with the chopped herbs, spinach and spring onions. Bring to the boil, then turn the heat to the lowest setting, put the lid on and simmer for 45 minutes.

Meanwhile, make the toppings and set aside.

Add the noodles to the soup and stir well to ensure that the noodles do not stick together. (If the *ash* is too thick, add a little boiling water.) Bring to the boil, then turn down the heat, put the lid on and simmer for 15 minutes, stirring from time to time. Taste and add salt if needed.

Stir the *kashk* into the soup, then ladle it into a large serving bowl or individual bowls. Swirl some *kashk* on top (mix with a tablespoon of water if the *kashk* is too thick to swirl), followed by the fried mint (including the oil in which it was cooked), crispy fried onions and crispy fried garlic toppings.

Note
For a quicker version of this soup, use a 400g tin of chickpeas and a 400g tin of pinto beans (rinsed and drained), adding them to the *ash* with the noodles. Use 2 litres of vegetable stock instead of 2.25 litres. (You won't need to simmer for 2¼ hours.)

PERSIAN TOMATO SOUP
ASH-E GOJEH FARANGI

SERVES 6

1kg ripe vine tomatoes, quartered

7 large garlic cloves, unpeeled

5 tbsp olive oil

Salt

2 large onions, finely chopped

1 tsp ground turmeric

½ tsp ground cumin

70g basmati rice, rinsed

½ tsp freshly ground black pepper

1.75 litres beef or vegetable stock

30g fresh flat-leaf parsley leaves, roughly chopped

35g fresh coriander, roughly chopped

25g fresh basil leaves, roughly chopped

40g fresh chives, roughly chopped

400g tinned plum tomatoes

50g good-quality tomato purée

FOR THE TOPPINGS

(see page 91)

3 tbsp dried mint for fried mint

3 onions for crispy fried onion (optional)

Olive and vegetable oil for frying

Tomato soup is popular in many countries, and this is a Persian version, which includes rice and fresh herbs, caramelized onions, turmeric and cumin. This combination of ingredients gives the soup a thick texture as well as a rich flavour.

Preheat the oven to 200°C/180°C fan/Gas 6 and line a baking tray with baking parchment.

Mix the tomatoes, garlic, 2 tablespoons of the olive oil and a pinch of salt in a large bowl, then transfer to the baking tray in a single layer. Roast for 45 minutes until semi-dried.

Meanwhile, add the remaining olive oil and the onions to a large heavy-based pan and fry on a medium heat for 12 minutes or until the onions are soft and golden brown; stir occasionally at first and more frequently as the onions begin to change colour to prevent them from burning. Add the turmeric and cumin and stir for a minute, then add the rice, black pepper and stock. Bring to the boil and then turn the heat to the lowest setting, put the lid on and simmer for 30 minutes.

By now the tomatoes should be ready.

Squeeze the garlic cloves out of their skins into the pan with the onions and rice and then add the roasted tomatoes, the chopped herbs, plum tomatoes and tomato purée. Using a hand blender, blitz until smooth and then bring to the boil. Turn the heat to the lowest setting, put the lid on and simmer for 15 minutes. Stir every now and then to prevent sticking.

Meanwhile, make the toppings and set aside.

To serve, ladle into bowls and swirl on some of the fried mint topping (including the oil in which it was cooked), plus some crispy fried onion if using.

POMEGRANATE SOUP WITH MEATBALLS
ASH-E ANAR

SERVES 6

50g fresh flat-leaf parsley
50g fresh coriander
40g fresh mint leaves
60g fresh chives
3 tbsp olive oil
3 large onions, finely chopped
½ tbsp ground turmeric
1 tsp ground cumin
1 tsp ground cinnamon
40g basmati rice, rinsed
80g dried yellow split peas, rinsed
60g pearl barley, rinsed
1 litre meat stock
1 litre pomegranate juice
100ml pomegranate molasses
Salt

FOR THE MEATBALLS

300g minced lamb (up to 20% fat)
1 onion, coarsely grated
1 tsp ground turmeric
½ tsp ground cumin
½ tsp ground cinnamon
¼ tsp freshly ground black pepper
½ tsp salt

FOR THE TOPPINGS

(see page 91)
3 tbsp dried mint for fried mint
3 onions for crispy fried onion (optional)
Olive and vegetable oil for frying
Pomegranate seeds (optional)

In Iran, people generally use sour pomegranate juice to make this soup. In this recipe I use sweet pomegranate juice combined with pomegranate molasses to give a sweet and sour taste. If you prefer it sweeter, add a little honey at the end. The fried mint topping gives this soup a wonderful flavour. For a vegetarian version, omit the meatballs and use vegetable stock instead.

Finely chop all the herbs, ideally in a food processor, and set aside.

In a large heavy-based pan, add the olive oil and the onions, stir to mix, and cook on a medium heat for 20 minutes until caramelized (do not rush this stage as the cooked onions form the base of the soup); stir occasionally at first and more frequently as the onions begin to change colour to prevent them from burning.

Add the turmeric, cumin and cinnamon, stir for 30 seconds, then add the rice, split peas, barley and stock. Bring to the boil, then turn the heat to the lowest setting, put the lid on and simmer for 40 minutes.

Meanwhile, make the meatballs: add all the ingredients to a large bowl and knead with your hand until evenly mixed, then shape into small meatballs (about 2–3cm in diameter). Set aside.

Add the chopped herbs, pomegranate juice and pomegranate molasses to the soup pan and stir well until fully mixed. Bring to the boil, add the meatballs, bring back to the boil and then turn the heat to the lowest setting, put the lid on and simmer for 50 minutes. Taste and adjust the seasoning if needed. Cook for a further 3 minutes on a medium heat without the lid.

While the soup is simmering, make the toppings and set aside.

To serve, garnish the soup with the fried mint topping (including the oil in which it was cooked), and crispy fried onion if using, and scatter over some pomegranate seeds if you like.

Trader, Imam Bazaar, Isfahan, Iran (April 2016)

RICE

PERSIAN RICE

Rice plays a central role in Iranian cuisine and is typically served with stews, kebabs and fish. The traditional method for cooking Persian rice is quite distinctive. It results in a fluffy texture with well-separated rice grains. It also has a delicious crispy base called *tahdig*, which translates as 'the bottom of the pot'. This is my favourite part of Persian rice. I've been asked many times how to create the crispy *tahdig*; the main advice that I give is to use a non-stick pan with a snug-fitting lid. Most importantly, creating the perfect *tahdig* requires practice.

There are two methods commonly used for cooking rice in Iran. The first method is called *chelow* or *pollow* and involves parboiling the rice before steaming it, to which may be added a layer of herbs, dried fruits, meat or beans. This method takes longer to prepare but results in fluffier rice and a much crunchier *tahdig*. The second method, which is called *kateh*, is easier and quicker to make and results in softer, less fluffy rice and a less crunchy *tahdig*.

SERVES 4–5

400g Persian rice (see page 13) or basmati rice
Salt
Butter
2 tbsp vegetable or light olive oil

CHELOW

Step 1: Washing the rice
Place the rice in a large bowl and fill with cold water. Swirl your fingers through the rice to release the starch and then change the water. Repeat this process two or three times until the water remains almost clear. Washing the rice removes starch and prevents the rice grains from becoming sticky.

Step 2: Soaking the rice (optional)
You need to follow this step if you are using Persian rice, but do not soak basmati rice. Refill the bowl with water, add 3 tablespoons of salt and mix. Soak for 4 to 12 hours (soaking the rice will elongate the grains and give it a fluffy texture). Drain the rice in a fine-mesh colander.

Step 3: Boiling and draining the rice
Half fill a non-stick pan with a snug-fitting lid (for this amount of rice I use a 20cm saucepan) with water, add 30g of butter and 2 tablespoons of salt. Bring the water to the boil and then add the drained rice. Stir the rice gently four or five times to prevent the grains from sticking together. Bring to the boil and boil for 3–5 minutes or until the grains start to float on top of the water and the colour changes from opaque to a more brilliant white; do not let the rice get fluffy or soft – when you bite a grain it should be firm and slightly hard in the centre. Drain the rice in a fine-mesh colander and pour two small glasses of cold water over the rice. Leave the rice in the colander for 2–3 minutes for the water to drain off.

Step 4: 'Tahdig' preparation
There are various types of *tahdig*, four of which I describe here – *rice tahdig*, *potato tahdig*, *yoghurt and saffron tahdig* and *flatbread tahdig*. In the same pan that you used to boil the rice, add 2 tablespoons of oil, a knob of butter, 2 tablespoons of water and a pinch of salt. Heat until the butter has melted and then remove the pan from the heat.

Rice tahdig: scatter a thin layer of the parboiled rice over the oil and butter to create a crispy base for the *tahdig* (see picture no.1 on page 114). If you wish, you can add a pinch of turmeric or saffron to the oil before scattering the rice on top.

Potato tahdig: peel 1–2 potatoes and slice into discs (approx. 5mm thick). Place a single layer of potato slices in the bottom of the pan on top of the oil and butter (see picture no.2 on page 114).

Yoghurt and saffron tahdig: grind a pinch of saffron threads in a pestle and mortar and then add 2 tablespoons of boiling water and leave to infuse for 5–10 minutes. Add 4 tablespoons of yoghurt and mix well, then add 5 heaped tablespoons of the parboiled rice and mix well. Place this mixture in the bottom of the pan on top of the oil and butter and gently press it down to form an even layer (see picture no.3 on page 114).

Flatbread tahdig: cut some extra-thin flatbread (no more than 2–3mm thick) or tortilla to fit the bottom of the pan. Place the disc of bread in the pan on top of the oil and butter (see picture no.4 on page 114).

Step 5: Scattering the rice on the tahdig

Scatter a layer of the parboiled rice on top of the *tahdig*, followed by another layer. Do not pack the layers of rice on top of each other as this will prevent the rice from fluffing up. Continue to scatter the rice until it is all used up, making a pyramid of rice (see picture no.5 on page 115).

The pyramid shape leaves room for the rice to expand. To release the steam, make four or five holes in the rice with the bottom of a wooden spoon. Scatter some flakes of butter on top of the rice (optional).

Step 6: Fitting the pan lid

Wrapping the lid of the pan helps to retain the steam, giving the rice a fluffy texture. Place a clean tea towel (see picture no.6 on page 115), or three or four layers of absorbent kitchen paper (see picture no.7 on page 115), on top of the pan and then put the lid on tightly. Tuck in the corners of the tea towel; if using kitchen paper, trim the edges to prevent the paper from catching fire. If the pan lid has a steam vent, make sure you cover the hole as you want the steam to build up in the pan (see picture no.7 on page 115). Place the lid on the pan, ensuring that it is tightly sealed to prevent the steam from escaping.

Step 7: Cooking method

Place the pan on a high heat for 5 minutes or until you see steam coming out from the edges of the lid; this will allow the steam to build up. Then reduce the heat to the lowest setting and cook for 50 minutes to 1 hour or until the grains are cooked and fluffed up and the base (*tahdig*) is crispy and golden (the timing may differ depending on the kind of cooker you are using because different cookers have different level of heat intensity). If the rice is still hard at the end of the recommended cooking time, then add 50ml of water to the pan, place the lid on tightly and cook for a further 15 minutes on the lowest setting.

Step 8: Serving the rice

To serve, turn the rice out onto a large plate as you might a cake (see picture no.8 on page 115). Alternatively, spoon the rice from the pan and remove the *tahdig* separately; this will be necessary if the rice has stuck to the bottom of the pan.

KATEH

Wash the rice (see step 1), drain, and add it to a 20cm non-stick saucepan with a snug-fitting lid. Add 650ml cold water, 1 teaspoon of salt and 20g of butter and bring to the boil. When it begins to boil, give it a good stir and place the lid on tightly, as described in step 6. Turn the heat to the lowest setting and cook for 40–50 minutes. If the rice is still hard at the end of the recommended cooking time, then add 50ml of water to the pan, place the lid on tightly and cook for a further 15 minutes on the lowest setting. Serve as described in step 8.

RICE WITH FRESH HERBS
SABZI POLOW

SERVES 4-5

60g fresh flat-leaf parsley leaves

60g fresh coriander

60g fresh dill leaves

60g fresh chives

400g basmati rice

Salt

Butter

Vegetable or light olive oil

1–2 potatoes, sliced (approx. 5mm thick) (optional)

This is traditionally served on Persian New Year or Nowruz (around 21 March) to celebrate the arrival of spring. The history of Nowruz, which translates to 'new day', dates back more than 3000 years; it's a day when families gather together. The green herbs in this dish symbolize the rebirth of nature. This is normally served with fish, which, in ancient Persian, symbolizes protection, good luck and prosperity.

Finely chop all the herbs, ideally in a food processor in batches, and set aside.

To prepare the rice, follow the first 3 steps on page 112, after which the rice will have been drained.

Add the chopped herbs to the rice and, using a rubber spatula, stir gently to prevent the rice grains from breaking, until the rice and herbs are fully mixed.

To cook the rice, follow steps 4 to 7 on page 112–113 (for step 4, choose either the *potato tahdig* to create a golden crispy potato base or the *rice tahdig*, scattering some of the rice and herbs mixture).

To serve: if your pan is completely non-stick, simply flip the rice onto a large plate as you might turn out a cake. Otherwise, use a large spoon and gently spoon out the rice into a serving dish, then remove the crispy golden *tahdig* and serve it on a separate plate.

BARBERRIES, PISTACHIOS AND ALMONDS IN SAFFRON WITH RICE
ZERESHK POLOW

SERVES 4

350g basmati rice

Salt

Butter

Light olive oil

3 generous pinches of saffron threads

Pinch of granulated or demerara sugar

1 large onion, finely chopped

100g dried barberries, rinsed (see page 12)

80g roasted flaked almonds

60g nibbed pistachios (or roughly chopped pistachios)

3 tbsp honey

Barberries are small, sweet and sour red berries. Dried barberries are used in many different recipes in Iran and *zereshk polow* is one of the most popular. It is often served at casual gatherings but also at larger dinner parties and weddings. Traditionally, it is served with various types of chicken, kebab or lamb shank (*khorak-e mahiche*, page 149).

First, start cooking the Persian rice (see pages 112–113).

Make the saffron water (see page 15) and set aside.

When the rice is nearly ready, start making the *zereshk* mix: melt 50g of butter with 1 tablespoon of olive oil in a large frying pan on a low to medium heat. Add the onion and stir to coat the onion in the butter. Fry for 10 minutes or until the onion is soft and light golden brown; stir occasionally at first and more frequently as the onion begins to change colour to prevent it from burning.

Add the barberries, almonds and pistachios (if the butter is unsalted then add a small pinch of salt) and cook for a minute or two, stirring constantly to prevent the barberries from burning (they will burn quickly). Add the honey and stir for 30 seconds, then add 2 more tablespoons of water to the saffron water before pouring onto the barberries mixture. Stir for 30 seconds or until all the water has evaporated. Set aside.

When the rice is ready, spoon onto a serving dish and add the *zereshk* mix on top; mix the *zereshk* and rice before eating. Alternatively, spoon the rice into the pan with the *zereshk* and stir gently to combine the rice with the barberries and nuts. Remove the *tahdig* and serve on a separate plate.

SAFFRON YOGHURT RICE CUPCAKES
TAH-CHIN

SERVES 4-6

300g chicken breast fillets, cut into 3cm pieces

1 onion, peeled and quartered

1 tsp ground turmeric

¼ tsp freshly ground black pepper

Salt

3–4 generous pinches of saffron threads

Pinch of granulated or demerara sugar

3 cardamom pods

40g butter, plus extra for greasing

300g Greek-style yoghurt (preferably full-fat)

¼ tsp ground cinnamon

1 egg

350g basmati rice

10g dried barberries, rinsed (see page 12), plus extra for topping

This saffron and yoghurt baked rice can be made in various ways and with different fillings, the most common of which is chicken. For a vegetarian version you can use dried barberries, baked aubergine or crispy fried onion (page 91). For best results use really thick Greek yoghurt.

Put the chicken in a saucepan and add 150ml water, the onion, turmeric, black pepper and a pinch of salt. Bring to the boil and then cover and simmer on the lowest setting for 20 minutes. Remove the lid, turn the heat up to high and cook for couple of minutes. Transfer the chicken to a plate to cool, then shred the meat and set aside. Reserve 3 tablespoons of the liquid.

Meanwhile, make the saffron water (see page 15) and set aside. Crack the cardamom pods in a mortar with a pestle to release the seeds. Discard the pods and grind the seeds to a fine powder; set aside. Melt 40g of butter and leave to cool.

In a large bowl, mix the yoghurt with the saffron water. Add the ground cardamom, cinnamon, ½ teaspoon of salt and the egg and stir thoroughly. Add the cooled melted butter, stir to mix, and set aside for the saffron to infuse in the yoghurt.

Preheat the oven to 200°C/180°C fan/Gas 6 and generously butter a 12-hole cupcake tin. Set aside.

To prepare the rice, follow the first 3 steps on page 112, after which the rice will have been drained.

Add the reserved chicken liquid to the bowl of yoghurt and mix. Then take 6 tablespoons of the yoghurt and mix with the shredded chicken. Set aside.

Now add your drained rice to the bowl of yoghurt and stir gently until fully mixed. Taste and season if needed.

Half fill each cupcake hole with rice and make a hollow in the centre. Divide the chicken mixture between the hollows and top with the barberries. Add another layer of rice to create a mound and sprinkle with barberries. Cover the cupcake tin with foil tightly and bake for 50–60 minutes or until the edges of the cupcakes are golden. Serve hot.

LENTILS WITH RICE AND CUMIN
ADAS POLOW

SERVES 4-5

200g green lentils, rinsed
1½ tsp salt
25g butter
1 tsp ground cumin
1 tsp ground cinnamon
250g basmati rice, rinsed
4 onions
Vegetable oil for frying

Adas polow is extremely popular throughout Iran and it has always been one of my favourite Iranian dishes. You can eat it without the crispy fried onion topping but I strongly recommend that you include it for extra flavour. *Adas polow* is traditionally served with chicken but it can also be served on its own or with a fried egg, a dollop of thick yoghurt on the side, or some pomegranate molasses on top.

Place the lentils, 1 litre of cold water and the salt in a saucepan. Bring to the boil and then turn the heat to low, put the lid on and simmer for 15–20 minutes or until the lentils are just tender to the bite but still holding their shape. Drain the lentils in a sieve over a bowl to catch the lentil water. Measure 600ml of the lentil water and set aside.

Melt the butter on a low heat in a large non-stick pan (about 24cm in diameter) with a snug-fitting lid and then add the cumin and cinnamon and stir well. Add the lentils and stir well to mix with the spices. Finally, add the rice and the reserved lentil water.

Mix well and bring to the boil. As soon as it starts to boil, put the lid on tightly (see step 6 on page 113).

Turn the heat to the lowest setting and cook for 40–50 minutes or until the rice is fully cooked. If the rice is still hard at the end of the recommended cooking time, then add 50ml of water to the pan, place the lid on tightly and cook for a further 15 minutes on the lowest setting.

While the rice is cooking, make the crispy fried onion topping (see page 91).

To serve, separate the grains of rice with a spoon and mix with the crispy fried onion. Spoon the rice onto a serving dish and then spoon out the *tahdig* from the bottom of the pan and serve on a separate plate.

HERBED RICE AND KOHLRABI WITH TINY MEATBALLS

KALAM POLOW BA KOOFTEH GHELGHELI

SERVES 4

30g fresh chives

30g fresh dill leaves

30g fresh tarragon leaves

800g peeled kohlrabi, cut into cubes (ideally 5mm, no bigger than 1cm cubes) or 700g finely shredded white cabbage

Salt

Butter

4 tbsp light olive oil

1½ tsp ground turmeric

¼ tsp ground cinnamon

¼ tsp ground cumin

50ml fresh lime juice

280g basmati rice

FOR THE MEATBALLS

300g minced lamb (up to 20% fat)

1 onion, coarsely grated

1 tsp ground turmeric

¼ tsp ground cinnamon

¼ tsp freshly ground black pepper

½ tsp salt

4 tbsp vegetable oil

This is one of my mom's signature recipes and when my friends visited our home when I was a child they would always ask her to cook this for them. It can also be served without the meatballs as a vegetarian dish, on its own or with pan-fried eggs or a dollop of yoghurt. It originated in Shiraz, a city of poetry and beautiful gardens and my parents' home town. You can find kohlrabi in most Middle Eastern supermarkets, but if it is not available then you can use white cabbage instead, although I do prefer to use kohlbari.

Finely chop all the herbs, ideally in a food processor, and set aside.

Place the kohlrabi or white cabbage in a large saucepan, add 1 litre cold water and 1 teaspoon of salt. Bring to the boil and simmer for 5 minutes or until cooked but still al dente. Drain and set aside.

In a large frying pan, melt 50g of butter and 1 tablespoon of the olive oil on a high heat. Add the drained kohlrabi/cabbage and fry for 12–15 minutes or until golden, stirring occasionally. Add the turmeric, cinnamon and cumin, mix well and cook for 1 minute, then add the lime juice and stir until all the juice has evaporated, add salt to taste and set aside.

To prepare the rice, follow the first 3 steps on page 112 (for step 3 use a 24cm pan instead of 20cm), after which the rice will have been drained. Add the chopped herbs to the drained rice and gently stir, using a rubber spatula, until the rice and herbs are fully mixed.

In the same pan that you used to boil the rice, add the remaining olive oil, a knob of butter, 2 tablespoons of water and a pinch of salt. Heat until the butter melts and then remove the pan from the heat. Scatter a layer of herbed rice on top, followed by a layer of kohlrabi/cabbage and another layer of herbed rice. Repeat this process until all the rice and kohlrabi/cabbage are used. Try not to make the layers

→

too thick (you should make four or five layers) and do not pack too tightly as this will prevent the rice from fluffing up.

Now follow steps 6 and 7 on page 113 to finish cooking the rice.

While the rice is cooking, make the meatballs: add the minced lamb, onion, turmeric, cinnamon, pepper and salt to a large bowl and knead with your hand, wash your hands and then shape into tiny meatballs (the size of a hazelnut). In a large frying pan (ideally non-stick), heat the vegetable oil on a medium heat until it is fully hot, gently add the meatballs (in batches if necessary) and fry for 4–6 minutes until brown and crisp. Set aside.

To serve, gently mix the layers of rice and kohlrabi before spooning into a serving dish. Add the meatballs on top of the rice. Remove the crispy *tahdig* from the bottom of the pan and serve on a separate plate.

Note
Just as pasta is central to Italian cuisine, so is rice a staple part of the diet in Iranian culture. It is not surprising, then, that it comes in many different varieties, including *domsiah*, *lenjan*, *tarom*, *kamfirooz* and *doodi*. The most popular varieties of rice originate from the north of Iran, largely due to the climate in that region. Aside from the wide variety of different kinds of rice, people use different methods to cook it. However, regardless of the cooking method, a unique feature of Iranian rice is the *tahdig*, which is a crispy base that can be created using potatoes, saffron yoghurt, bread or rice itself. It takes practice to create the perfect *tahdig* and, despite my many years of cooking it, I still find myself refining my technique. The type of pan you use, the variety of rice you are cooking and the intensity of the heat can all determine the quality of the *tahdig*.

PRAWNS, BARBERRIES AND SAFFRON WITH RICE
MEIGU POLOW

SERVES 4

350g basmati rice

Salt

Butter

Light olive oil

2 generous pinches of saffron threads

Pinch of granulated or demerara sugar

500g raw peeled prawns

1 large onion, finely chopped

90g dried barberries, rinsed (see page 12)

120g tiny raisins (or larger raisins, roughly chopped)

Meigu polow is a very popular dish from the south of Iran, close to the Persian Gulf. I remember my grandmother making this dish when we used to visit her in the city of Shiraz. The traditional recipe uses very tiny prawns but you can use regular prawns, cut in half lengthways.

First, start cooking the Persian rice (see pages 112–113).

Make the saffron water (see page 15) and set aside.

Cut the prawns in half lengthways into two pieces and remove any veins.

When the rice is nearly ready, melt 30g of butter in a large frying pan on a medium heat. Add 1 tablespoon of olive oil and the onion (if the butter is unsalted, add a pinch of salt) and, using a wooden spoon, stir to coat the onions in the butter and oil. Stirring frequently, fry for 10 minutes or until soft and golden.

Add the barberries and raisins and stir constantly for 1 minute. Add the prawns and cook until they are almost done, stirring constantly to avoid burning the barberries.

Add 2 more tablespoons of water to the saffron water and then pour over the prawns, stirring well so that the saffron water mixes fully with the prawns. Cook further until all the water evaporates and the prawns are fully cooked, stirring constantly. Remove from the heat and cover with foil until the rice is ready.

To serve, spoon some rice onto a serving plate, add some of the prawn mixture on top and mix before eating. Alternatively, add the rice to the pan with the prawns, stir well, then serve.

Note
If you wish, you can use 2 onions to prepare the crispy fried onion topping (see page 91) to add to this dish.

RICE WITH BROAD BEANS AND DILL
BAGHALI POLOW

SERVES 4

400g podded broad beans (fresh or frozen)

Salt

Butter

½ tsp ground cumin

½ tsp ground cinnamon

½ tsp garlic powder

280g basmati rice

35g fresh dill leaves, finely chopped

Vegetable or light olive oil

1–2 potatoes, sliced (approx. 5mm thick)

This is a Persian classic, combining the flavours of dill and broad beans. It is often served at weddings and you can find it in almost all Iranian restaurants. It is usually served with *khorak-e mahiche* (page 149), a traditional Iranian dish of lamb shanks. It can also be served with pan-fried fish (page 193), fried egg or simply with a dollop of thick yoghurt. I like to use baby broad beans even though they take longer to prepare.

Place the broad beans, ½ teaspoon of salt and 500ml of boiling water in a saucepan, bring to the boil and cook for 3–6 minutes or until the beans float in the water and are tender (cooking time will depend on the size and tenderness of the beans). Drain in a colander and rinse under cold running water to prevent the beans from cooking further. Squeeze the beans out of their skins, split the large beans in two and set aside.

Melt 25g of butter in a large frying pan, turn off the heat and add the cumin, cinnamon, garlic powder and the broad beans (if the butter is unsalted, add a pinch of salt). Stir well to coat the broad beans in the butter and spices. Set aside.

To prepare the rice, follow the first 3 steps on page 112, after which the rice will have been drained.

Add the rice and the dill to the broad beans and gently stir, using a rubber spatula, until fully mixed.

To cook the rice, follow steps 4 to 7 on pages 112–113 (for step 4, choose the *potato tahdig*).

To serve, gently spoon out the rice into a serving dish. Remove the crispy *tahdig* and serve on a separate plate.

RICE WITH GREEN BEANS AND LAMB
LUBIA POLOW

SERVES 4-5

3 generous pinches of saffron threads

Pinch of granulated or demerara sugar

Light olive oil

1 large onion, finely chopped

1 tsp ground turmeric

1 tsp ground cumin

1 tsp ground cinnamon

450g boneless leg of lamb or neck fillet, cut into 1.5–2cm pieces

380g green beans, trimmed and cut into 2cm pieces

Salt

150g good-quality tomato purée

80ml fresh lime juice

350g basmati rice

Butter

Lubia Polow is hugely popular in Iran. I often serve it at home and it is always a big hit with my guests. For a vegetarian version, omit the meat and add the beans with 150ml of boiling water after adding the spices to the onion.

Make the saffron water (see page 15). Set aside.

Add the onion and 2 tablespoons of olive oil to a large frying pan and fry for about 5 minutes until the onion is soft and golden brown. Add the turmeric, cumin and ½ teaspoon of the cinnamon and stir well.

Add the meat and cook, stirring frequently, for about 5 minutes until the meat is almost cooked, then add 300ml boiling water, stir and bring to the boil. Turn the heat to low to medium, put the lid on and simmer for 15 minutes.

Add the beans, stir well and bring back to the boil, then turn the heat down, cover and simmer for a further 10 minutes, stir in a good pinch of salt, and cook uncovered until all the water has evaporated.

In a small saucepan, mix 2 tablespoons of olive oil with the remaining cinnamon and the tomato purée and cook on a medium heat for 2 minutes, stirring constantly.

Add the tomato purée mixture, the saffron water and lime juice to the bean mixture and mix well, turn up the heat and cook until all the liquid has evaporated. Taste and season if needed.

To prepare the rice, follow the first 4 steps on pages 112–113 (for step 3 use a 24cm pan instead of 20cm, and for step 4, choose the *rice tahdig*).

At this point, you should have a layer of rice at the bottom of your pan. Spoon in a layer of bean mixture followed by a layer of rice. Repeat this process until all the rice and bean mixture are used. Try not to make the layers too thick (you should make four or five layers) and do not pack too tightly.

Now follow steps 6 and 7 on page 113 to finish cooking the rice.

To serve, use a large spoon to mix the rice, meat and beans and then spoon onto a serving dish. Remove the *tahdig* and place on a separate plate.

Mountain of salt by the salt lake, Shiraz, Iran (April 2015)

Kazerun Fruit Bazaar, Kazerun, Iran (April 2017)

STEWS

PERSIAN DAL
DAL ADAS

SERVES 4

3 tbsp vegetable or light olive oil

3 large onions, finely chopped

1 large bulb of garlic, cloves separated and crushed

½ tbsp ground turmeric

½ tsp ground cumin

¼ tsp ground cinnamon

200g red lentils, rinsed

750ml vegetable stock

1 large potato (about 250g), peeled and chopped into roughly 1cm cubes

30g good-quality tomato purée

2 tbsp fresh lime juice

¼–1 tsp chilli powder

Salt

Chopped fresh coriander and red chilli to garnish (optional)

Persian dal, a vegetarian dish, is easy to make and very tasty. Although it looks a little like Indian dal, the combination of ingredients is quite different. *Dal adas* originated in the city of Bushehr in the south of Iran, on the Persian Gulf. It is usually served with Persian rice (pages 112–113).

Add the oil and onions to a large pan on a medium heat and fry for 10–12 minutes, stirring occasionally, until soft and beginning to turn golden brown.

Add the garlic and cook for 3 minutes, stirring constantly. Add the turmeric, cumin and cinnamon and stir for 30 seconds before adding the lentils and mixing well.

Add the stock, stir, and bring to the boil. Reduce the heat to the lowest setting, cover with a lid and simmer for 15 minutes.

Add the chopped potatoes, give it a good stir, put the lid back on and cook for a further 20–25 minutes or until the potatoes are tender, stirring every now and then to prevent the ingredients from sticking to the bottom of the pan.

Add the tomato purée, lime juice and chilli powder to taste and stir well. Taste and add salt if needed. Cook on a medium heat for a couple of minutes without the lid (if the texture is too thick, add a little boiling water). Scatter over some chopped coriander and chilli, if using, and serve.

SLOW-COOKED LAMB WITH FRESH HERBS AND BEANS

GHORMEH SABZI

SERVES 4

- 6 tbsp vegetable or light olive oil
- 1 large red onion, finely chopped
- 1 tsp ground turmeric
- 400–600g boneless leg of lamb, cut into 3cm pieces
- ¼ tsp freshly ground black pepper
- 120g fresh flat-leaf parsley
- 120g fresh coriander
- 120g fresh chives
- 100g fresh spinach leaves
- 1 tbsp dried fenugreek (see page 12)
- 400g tin of red kidney beans, rinsed and drained
- 4 Persian dried limes (see page 13)
- Salt
- 60ml fresh lime juice

This stew, which is often referred to as the king of Persian stews, is extremely popular in Iran and is served in almost all Iranian restaurants. The combination of fresh herbs and slow-cooked lamb, soft beans and the tanginess of dried limes makes this stew especially flavoursome. It is usually served with Persian rice (pages 112–113). Instead of boneless meat, you can use meat on the bone, which gives an even better flavour.

Add 2 tablespoons of the oil and the chopped onion to a large, heavy-based pan on a medium heat and fry for 5–7 minutes until the onion is soft and translucent and beginning to turn golden brown. Add the turmeric and stir to mix.

Add the meat and stir for a couple of minutes or until the meat is no longer red. Add 750ml freshly boiled water and the pepper and bring to the boil, then turn the heat down to the lowest setting, put the lid on and simmer for 2 hours.

Meanwhile, finely chop all the herbs and the spinach, ideally in a food processor in batches.

Add the remaining oil and the chopped herbs and spinach to a large frying pan on a medium heat and fry for 10 minutes, stirring constantly. Add the fenugreek and stir for a further 2 minutes and then set aside.

Add the fried herbs to the pan of meat, along with the kidney beans, dried limes and salt to taste, bring back to the boil and then cook with the lid on for 30 minutes on the lowest setting.

Add the lime juice, taste and add more salt if needed and cook on a medium heat without the lid for a further 3–5 minutes or until the stew has thickened slightly. Serve.

PERSIAN MEATBALLS IN TOMATO AND HERB SAUCE

KOOFTEH BERENJI

MAKES 8

70g yellow split peas, rinsed
Salt
70g basmati rice, rinsed
15g fresh flat-leaf parsley
15g fresh coriander
15g fresh tarragon leaves
10g fresh dill leaves
15g fresh chives
500g minced lamb (up to 20% fat)
1 small red onion, coarsely grated
2 tsp ground turmeric
2 tsp ground cumin
½ tsp ground cinnamon
¼ tsp chilli powder
½ tsp freshly ground black pepper
2 large garlic cloves, crushed
25g barberries, rinsed (see page 12)
2 eggs
16–24 no-soak pitted prunes

FOR THE BROTH

15g fresh chives
15g fresh coriander
10g fresh dill leaves
2 tbsp olive oil
1 onion, finely chopped
100g good-quality tomato purée
¼ tsp ground turmeric
¼ tsp ground cumin
¼ tsp ground cinnamon
150g cherry tomatoes, cut in half
¼ tsp salt

Koofteh, which is a meatball dish, is made in different ways in different regions of Iran. For example, when I was studying at the University of Tabriz in the north-west of Iran, my friend's mother used to make a single large meatball (almost as big as a football), inside of which she would place an entire small chicken as a filling. This recipe makes eight small meatballs and for the filling I have used prunes, which give the meatballs a soft and juicy texture. However, you can use other fillings like raisins and walnuts or hardboiled quail eggs. Regardless of the kind of filling you are using, it is common to add crispy fried onions (see page 91) to your filling (for this recipe 1 onion should suffice).

Place the split peas and 750ml cold water in a small saucepan, add 1 teaspoon of salt and bring to the boil. Discard the foam on the surface of the water, reduce the heat and simmer on a low heat for 40–50 minutes or until cooked. The split peas should still be al dente and holding their shape. Drain and leave to cool completely.

Add 500ml freshly boiled water to a small saucepan, add 1 teaspoon salt and the rice. Bring to the boil and cook for 6–8 minutes or until the rice is completely cooked and soft but not mushy. Drain and leave to cool completely.

Meanwhile, finely chop all the herbs for the *koofteh*, ideally in a food processor, and set aside, then finely chop all the herbs for the broth and set aside.

In a large bowl, add the herbs for the *koofteh* along with the cold cooked split peas and the rice. Add the lamb, onion, turmeric, cumin, cinnamon, chilli, black pepper, garlic, barberries, eggs and 1 teaspoon of salt. Using your hands, knead for about 5 minutes or until evenly mixed and sticky.

Wet your hands and then divide the meat mixture into eight equal pieces. Shape one of the pieces into a ball. Using your finger, make a hole halfway into the meatball and add 2 or 3 prunes, pushing them into the middle →

of the meatball. Reshape the meatball and briefly give it a firm squeeze to make sure it will not open during cooking; set aside on a tray. Repeat this process until you have used all the meat mixture.

To make the broth, add the oil and onion to a large heavy-based pan (approximately 25cm – large enough to hold all the meatballs in a single layer) and fry on a medium heat for about 5 minutes until golden. Add the tomato purée, stirring for 3 minutes. Add the turmeric, cumin, cinnamon, tomatoes, salt and the reserved herbs. Add 1.1 litres of freshly boiled water, stir and bring to the boil. One by one, place the meatballs carefully into the pan and cook for 1 hour on a low to medium heat with the lid on, slightly ajar.

With a large spoon, carefully turn the meatballs over and cook on a low heat, without the lid, for a further 15 minutes.

To serve, transfer the meatballs to a large dish. If you wish, you can simply pour the meatball juice over the meatballs and serve with a flat bread or barbary bread (see page 201). Alternatively, you can serve this dish the way it is commonly served in Iran. This involves transferring the meatball juice to a large bowl and breaking some bread into small pieces, which you then soak in the meatball juice until soft before eating with the meatballs.

Old bread-baking room, Boldaji, Iran (May 2018)

LAMB SHANKS WITH SAFFRON
KHORAK-E MAHICHE

SERVES 4

1 red onion, finely chopped
1 tbsp olive oil
1 tsp ground turmeric
1 tsp ground cumin
½ tsp ground cinnamon
½ tsp freshly ground black pepper
4 lamb shanks, fat trimmed
2 vine tomatoes, quartered
2 generous pinches of saffron threads
Pinch of granulated or demerara sugar
50g good-quality tomato purée
40ml fresh lime juice
Salt

Khorak-e mahiche is one of the most popular dishes in Iran and is served with various rice dishes, especially *baghali polow* (page 129). *Khorak-e mahiche*, which is often served at parties and weddings, is usually cooked on a hob, but I find the meat is more tender when cooked in the oven. If you buy your lamb shank from a butcher's shop, ask your butcher to trim off the fat to prevent a layer of fat forming on top of the *khorak-e mahiche*. I recommend that you pour some of the juice from the lamb shank onto the accompanying rice and *tahdig* to enrich its flavour.

Preheat the oven to 160°C/140°C fan/Gas 3.

In a large flameproof casserole dish, add the onion and oil and fry on a medium heat for about 5 minutes until the onion is soft and just turning golden. Add the turmeric, cumin, cinnamon and black pepper and stir well, then add the lamb shanks and cook for a couple of minutes until lightly browned (be careful not to burn the spices).

Add the tomatoes and 550ml freshly boiled water and bring to the boil. Put the lid on the dish, transfer to the oven and cook for 2½ hours.

Meanwhile, make the saffron water (see page 15) and set aside.

When the lamb shanks are cooked and tender, remove the dish from the oven. Add a ladleful of the lamb juice to the bowl of saffron water and then add the tomato purée, lime juice and salt to taste. Stir to mix, pour over the lamb, and place the dish (without the lid) back in the oven for a further 30 minutes before serving.

YELLOW SPLIT PEAS WITH LAMB, TOPPED WITH ROASTED AUBERGINE

GHEIMEH BADEMJAN

SERVES 4

200g yellow split peas

2 generous pinches of saffron threads

Pinch of granulated or demerara sugar

2 large onions, cut in half and then finely sliced into half-moon shapes

Olive oil

1½ tsp ground turmeric

½ tsp ground cumin

½ tsp ground cinnamon

¼ tsp freshly ground black pepper

400–600g lamb neck fillet, sliced into 2cm pieces

2 large aubergines, peeled and sliced lengthways into 1cm-thick slices, soaked if necessary (see page 12)

4 Persian dried limes (see page 13)

60g good-quality tomato purée

60ml fresh lime juice

Salt

When I was at university in Tabriz, in the north-west of Iran, my flatmate's grandmother used to make the best *gheimeh bademjan* when she visited us from Tehran. I am using her recipe. In Iran, matchstick fries are often added on top to add flavour, but this is optional. Note that the cooking time will vary depending on the freshness of the peas you use – if possible, use freshly bought peas. In this recipe I have used boneless meat but, like other recipes in this chapter, you can also use meat on the bone, such as leg of lamb or shoulder on the bone. If you do use meat on the bone then first remove the bone from the meat either yourself or ask your butcher to do so and cut into pieces. Keep the bone to add to the stew at the same time that you add the meat. When the stew is ready to serve you can discard the bone. This will enrich the flavour of the stew, which is usually served with Persian rice (pages 112–113). I sometimes alter this dish for my vegetarian friends by omitting the meat, adding vegetable stock instead of water and increasing the number of aubergines by one or two.

Soak the peas in a bowl of water and set aside. Make the saffron water (see page 15) and set aside.

Add the onions and 4 tablespoons of olive oil to a large heavy-based pan, stir to mix, and fry on a medium heat for 20 minutes or until the onions are soft and the edges are golden brown. Stir occasionally at first and more frequently as the onions begin to change colour.

Add the turmeric, cumin, cinnamon and black pepper and stir well, then add the meat and fry for a couple of minutes. Add 850ml freshly boiled water, bring to the boil and then put the lid on and simmer on the lowest setting for 1 hour.

Meanwhile, preheat the oven to 200°C/180°C fan/Gas 6 and line a baking tray with baking parchment.

→

Brush the aubergine slices generously with olive oil on both sides and sprinkle with a little salt. Place on the lined tray in a single layer and bake for 35–40 minutes or until the edges are golden brown. Set aside.

Drain the peas and add to the meat pan along with the dried limes and a good pinch of salt, bring to the boil and then turn the heat down to the lowest setting, put the lid on and simmer for 50 minutes–1¼ hours or until the peas are fully cooked: they should be just tender to the bite but still holding their shape.

Add the tomato purée, lime juice and saffron water and stir to mix. Taste the stew and season if needed. At this point, if you wish to bring out the flavour of the dried lime further, you can press each of the dried limes against the side of the pan to release the lime juice. You can either dispose of the dried limes or leave them in the stew. Stir the stew one more time and taste. Adjust the seasoning if needed and then add the baked aubergines on top in layers. Cook the stew on a medium heat without the lid for 5–10 minutes: the aubergines will soak up the juice and the liquid will thicken. Serve with matchstick fries on top if you like.

Matchstick fries

Peel 1 large potato, cut into matchstick-size pieces and sprinkle with salt. Heat 4–5 tablespoons of oil in a frying pan on a medium heat; when the oil is very hot, add the potatoes (in two batches if necessary) and fry until they are golden and crispy. Drain on kitchen paper.

LAMB SHANKS WITH QUINCE AND PRUNES
KHOROSHT-E BEH

SERVES 4

2 generous pinch of saffron threads
Pinch of granulated or demerara sugar
20g butter
2 onions, finely chopped
½ tbsp ground turmeric
1 tsp ground cinnamon
1 tsp ground cumin
¼ tsp ground ginger
4 lamb shanks, fat trimmed
120g yellow split peas, rinsed
2 quinces, cored and each cut into 8 wedges
10 no-soak pitted prunes
4 Persian dried limes (see page 13)
60ml fresh lime juice
800ml beef stock
Salt

Quince is an ancient fruit, grown in Iran and Turkey and across South-East Asia. The quince and prunes give a fruity taste to this sweet and sour stew. For best results, ask your butcher to trim the excess fat from the lamb shank, otherwise you are likely to end up with too much fat on top of the stew. This is best served with Persian rice (pages 112–113), or you can also have it with mashed potato.

Make the saffron water (see page 15) and set aside.

Preheat the oven to 160°C/140°C fan/Gas 3.

Melt the butter in a large flameproof casserole dish on a medium heat, then add the onions and cook for 10 minutes until soft and lightly golden, stirring occasionally at first and more frequently as the onions begin to change colour. Add the turmeric, cinnamon, cumin and ginger and stir well, then add the lamb shanks and fry for about 2 minutes, turning frequently, until the meat is lightly browned (be careful not to burn the spices).

Add the split peas, quinces, prunes, dried limes, half of the lime juice and the stock and bring to the boil. Put the lid on, place the dish in the oven, and cook for 2½ hours.

Remove the dish from the oven, add the saffron water and the remaining lime juice. Place the dish back in the oven without the lid for a further 30 minutes. Taste and season if needed before serving.

If the stew is too runny, boil on a high heat until it thickens, then serve.

CHICKEN WITH CARROTS, PRUNES AND SAFFRON
KHOROSHT-E ALOO

SERVES 4

3 generous pinches of saffron threads

Pinch of granulated or demerara sugar

1 tbsp olive oil

1 large onion, finely chopped

1 tsp ground turmeric

¼ tsp ground cinnamon

1kg skinless chicken drumsticks and thighs on the bone

Salt

¼ tsp freshly ground black pepper

Small pinch of chilli powder

150g golden prunes (see page 12), no-soak pitted prunes or no-soak dried apricots

40g shelled walnuts, roughly chopped

200g baby carrots, or 200g medium-sized carrots cut into 2cm pieces

30ml pomegranate molasses

½ to 1 tsp honey (optional)

This sweet and sour stew reminds me of lunchtime at my grandmother's house in Isfahan where she would serve it as a special treat; I have included it here in her memory. If you use apricots in this recipe I recommend that you look for some that are not preserved with sulphur dioxide. This stew is easy to make and is great with Persian rice (pages 112–113); pour some of the juice from the stew over the rice to add flavour.

Make the saffron water (see page 15) and set aside.

Add the oil and onion to a heavy-based pan on a medium heat and cook for 5–7 minutes until the onion is translucent and lightly golden.

Add the turmeric and cinnamon and mix well, then add the chicken and fry until it is lightly golden all over. Add a small pinch of salt, the black pepper and a small pinch of chilli powder.

Add 300ml freshly boiled water, bring to the boil, then turn the heat down to the lowest setting, put the lid on and simmer for 45 minutes.

Add the prunes, walnuts and carrots, bring back to the boil, cover and simmer on the lowest setting for another 40 minutes.

Remove about half of the prunes, put them in a small bowl and mash with the back of a spoon. Add the pomegranate molasses, saffron water and 1 ladleful of the chicken liquid, stir to mix and then stir into the stew. Taste and adjust the seasoning, adding honey if needed (this may depend on the sourness of the pomegranate molasses), bring back to the boil and cook on a medium heat for a further 5 minutes without the lid. This will allow the liquid to thicken and the flavours to blend. If you find that the stew is too runny, boil for a little longer but do not let the liquid evaporate completely because it is nice to pour some of the juice onto the rice.

AUBERGINE AND OKRA STEW
KHOROSHT-E BADEMJAN

SERVES 4

3–4 aubergines (1–1.2kg total weight), peeled and sliced lengthways into 1cm-thick slices, soaked if necessary (see page 12)

Light olive oil

Salt

2 generous pinches of saffron threads

Pinch of granulated or demerara sugar

400–600g lamb neck fillet or boneless leg of lamb, cut into 4cm pieces, or 4 skinless chicken legs

2 vine tomatoes, cut into quarters

1 large onion, peeled and cut in half

1 tsp ground turmeric

½ tsp ground cinnamon

¼ tsp freshly ground black pepper

170g okra

Salt

100g good-quality tomato purée

80ml fresh lime juice

Khorosht-e bademjan is a classic Persian stew. It is usually made with lamb, but chicken is also delicious. Adding okra gives the stew a thick texture and distinctive flavour. This is great with Persian rice (pages 112–113), and I like to add a generous amount of juice from the stew to my rice.

Preheat the oven to 200°C/180°C fan/Gas 6 and line a baking tray with baking parchment. Brush the aubergine slices generously with olive oil and sprinkle with a little salt. Place in a single layer on the baking tray and bake for 35–40 minutes or until the edges are golden brown. Set aside.

While the aubergine is baking, make the saffron water (see page 15) and set aside.

Meanwhile, in a large (ideally 24cm diameter) heavy-based shallow pan, add the lamb or chicken, tomatoes, onion, turmeric, half of the cinnamon, the black pepper and cold water (370ml for lamb, 300ml for chicken) and stir well. Bring to the boil, put the lid on and simmer on the lowest setting for 2 hours for lamb, 1 hour for chicken.

Discard the onion and add the okra and a good pinch of salt, bring back to the boil, put the lid back on and cook on the lowest setting for a further 20 minutes.

Meanwhile, in a small saucepan mix the tomato purée, 1 tablespoon of oil and the remaining cinnamon and cook for couple of minutes on a medium heat, stirring constantly.

Add the tomato purée mixture, lime juice, 50ml boiling water and a pinch of salt to the saffron water. Mix well and then pour half of it into the lamb/chicken pan and stir to mix. Taste and adjust the seasoning, then remove 3 ladlefuls of the stew liquid and mix with the remaining tomato and saffron mix, stir and set aside.

Add the roasted aubergines to the pan, laying the slices on top of the meat. Pour the remaining tomato and saffron mix evenly over the aubergines.

Bring back to the boil and boil on a medium to high heat for 5–7 minutes or until the liquid thickens. Serve.

CHICKEN WITH WALNUTS AND POMEGRANATE MOLASSES
FESENJAN

SERVES 4

250g shelled walnuts
1 tbsp vegetable oil
1 large onion, finely chopped
¼ tsp ground turmeric
8 skinless chicken thighs, on the bone
Salt
200ml pomegranate molasses
½–1 tbsp honey
Pomegranate seeds to garnish (optional)

This popular dish is originally from northern Iran, which has a large population of wild ducks. It is not surprising then that the original *fesenjan* recipe was made with duck. However, these days most people use chicken. The contrasting flavours of walnuts and pomegranate combine to give this dish a rich sweet and sour taste and a nutty texture. It is best served with Persian rice (pages 112–113).

Finely grind the walnuts in a food processor until the walnut crumbs begin to stick together.

Put the ground walnuts in a large heavy-based pan and roast on a medium heat, stirring constantly, for 4–5 minutes or until you begin to get the scent of the walnuts. Add 420ml cold water and stir well, bring to the boil, put the lid on and simmer on the lowest setting for 1 hour.

Meanwhile, add the oil and onion to a large frying pan on a medium heat and cook for 5–7 minutes until the onion is translucent and lightly golden. Add the turmeric and mix well, then add the chicken and fry until it is lightly golden all over. Add a small pinch of salt and set aside.

When the walnuts are ready, add the pomegranate molasses and honey to sweeten to your taste (this may depend on the sourness of the pomegranate molasses), stir until completely mixed and then add the chicken (including the onion) to the walnut mixture. Bring to the boil, then turn the heat down to the lowest setting, put the lid on and simmer for 1½ hours, stirring every now and then to ensure the walnuts at the bottom of the pan have become fully integrated into the stew. This will prevent the walnuts from sticking to the bottom of the pan. At the end of the cooking time, a layer of oil from the walnuts should have formed on the surface of the stew, and the colour should have turned dark.

Remove the lid, increase the heat to medium and boil for about 3–5 minutes or until the liquid thickens, stirring every now and then. Taste and add more honey if needed.

Serve, garnished with pomegranate seeds if you like.

CHICKEN WITH ORANGE JUICE AND BARBERRIES

MORGH BA PORTEGHAL

SERVES 4

Generous pinch of saffron threads

Pinch of granulated or demerara sugar

1 tbsp olive oil

1 onion, finely chopped

8 skinless chicken thighs, on the bone

½ tsp ground turmeric

¼ tsp ground cumin

Salt

150ml freshly squeezed orange juice

15g dried barberries, rinsed (see page 12)

This slow-cooked chicken dish can be served with various types of rice, including those in the rice chapter of this book (apart from *lubia polow*). The orange juice and barberries give the dish a sweet and sour flavour and help to tenderize the chicken.

Make the saffron water (see page 15) and set aside.

Add the oil and onion to a large heavy-based pan on a medium heat and cook for 5–7 minutes until the onion is translucent and lightly golden. Add the chicken and fry until lightly golden all over.

Add the turmeric, cumin and a good pinch of salt and stir for a minute.

Add the orange juice and 200ml freshly boiled water, bring to the boil, put the lid on and cook on the lowest setting for 1¼ hours.

Add the barberries and saffron water and cook for a further 20 minutes. Remove the lid, increase the heat to medium to high and boil for 5–7 minutes or until the liquid thickens. Serve.

COD WITH FRESH HERBS, GARLIC AND TAMARIND

GHALYEH MAHI

SERVES 4

150g fresh coriander

70g fresh flat-leaf parsley

5 tbsp vegetable or light olive oil

½ tbsp dried fenugreek (see page 12)

100g tamarind paste

2 large red onions, finely chopped

8 large garlic cloves, crushed

½ tbsp ground turmeric

¼–1 tsp chilli powder

600g skinless cod fillet, cut into 5cm pieces

Salt (optional)

This recipe, which originates from the south of Iran, is one of my grandma's specialities. I have made a few changes because the tamarind that is available in Iran is quite different from the tamarind available in most western countries. The fried herbs and garlic, tamarind paste and chilli combine to create a hot, aromatic and sour sauce in which the cod is cooked. If you prefer, you can use prawns instead of cod but remember to reduce the cooking time accordingly. This dish is usually served with Persian rice (pages 112–113).

Finely chop the coriander and parsley, ideally in a food processor. Place the herbs and 3 tablespoons of the oil in a large non-stick frying pan on a medium heat and fry, stirring constantly, for 7–10 minutes or until the colour has changed to dark green. Add the fenugreek and stir for a minute, then set aside.

Mix the tamarind paste with 400ml boiling water until completely mixed and set aside.

In a large saucepan, fry the onions with the remaining oil on a medium heat for 15 minutes until soft and golden brown. Add the garlic and cook, stirring constantly, for 2–3 minutes or until the garlic is lightly golden (do not let the garlic burn or it will make the stew bitter).

Add the turmeric and stir for 30 seconds. Add the tamarind water, fried herbs and chilli powder to taste. Stir well. Bring to the boil and then turn the heat to the lowest setting, put the lid on and simmer for 20 minutes.

Add the cod to the pan and cover with the stew. Bring back to the boil and then turn the heat to the lowest setting and simmer, with the lid on, for 15 minutes.

Taste and add salt if needed. Leave on a medium heat without the lid for a couple of minutes before serving.

Qur'an Gate, Shiraz, Iran (March 2015)

Trader, Vakil Bazaar, Shiraz, Iran (April 2017)

KEBABS, ROASTS & GRILLS

PAN KEBAB WITH TOMATO AND MUSHROOM SAUCE

KABAB BOSHGHABI

SERVES 4

2 generous pinches of saffron threads (optional)

Pinch of granulated or demerara sugar (optional)

80g good-quality tomato purée

60ml fresh lime juice

Salt

35g fresh flat-leaf parsley

500g minced lamb (up to 20% fat)

1 large onion, coarsely grated

½ tbsp ground turmeric

1 tsp ground cumin

½ tsp ground cinnamon

½ tsp freshly ground black pepper

2 tbsp olive oil

200g mushrooms, thinly sliced

150g cherry tomatoes

This Persian dish represents a rather casual approach to making kebab in Iran. I remember my mother making this dish when she didn't have much time to do the kind of preparation that is generally required to make kebab. It is one of my favourite childhood dishes and, although it goes well with most types of rice, it is traditionally served with *kateh* (see page 113), mashed potato, or some kind of bread on the side.

If using, make the saffron water (see page 15) and set aside.

To make the tomato sauce, combine the tomato purée, lime juice, saffron water if using, a pinch of salt and 50ml water in a small bowl and stir well. Set aside.

Finely chop the parsley, ideally in a food processor. Set aside.

In a large bowl, combine the meat, onion, chopped parsley, turmeric, cumin, cinnamon, black pepper and ½ teaspoon of salt. Using your hand, knead until all the ingredients are completely mixed.

Add the olive oil to a large frying pan (about 30cm in diameter, ideally non-stick) and, using your hand, flatten the meat evenly on the bottom of the pan. Put the pan on a medium heat for about 8 minutes or until the bottom of the meat has browned and most of the liquid has evaporated.

Cut the meat into four equal pieces and then flip each piece over.

Spread the mushrooms over the meat, followed by the cherry tomatoes, then pour the tomato sauce evenly on top.

Place the lid on the pan and cook for 7 minutes or until the mushrooms are cooked and the tomatoes burst. Remove the lid and cook until the water has evaporated and the other side of the meat is golden brown. Serve.

PERSIAN STUFFED AUBERGINE

DOLMEH BADEMJAN

SERVES 4

4 aubergines (about 250–300g each)

5 tbsp vegetable oil

3 tbsp olive oil

120g green beans, trimmed and cut into 1cm pieces

Salt

2 onions, finely chopped

3 large garlic cloves, finely chopped

1 tsp ground turmeric

1 tsp ground cumin

½ tsp freshly ground black pepper

Pinch of chilli powder

300g minced lamb (up to 20% fat)

80g good-quality tomato purée

50ml fresh lime juice

1 large vine tomato (about 200g), finely chopped

40g fresh coriander, finely chopped

15g fresh tarragon leaves, finely chopped

2–3 tbsp toasted flaked almonds to garnish (optional)

When I make this dish, I am reminded of my student days in the city of Tabriz, in the north-west of Iran. My landlord often made stuffed aubergines and, knowing that I had a fondness for them, would kindly bring some to me in the evenings after a long day at university. What distinguishes this from other stuffed aubergine recipes is the method of stuffing the whole aubergine, and the lime juice and herbs give a distinctive flavour to the meat. This recipe is commonly served with a piece of bread on the side.

Taking care not to remove the stalks and crowns, peel strips of skin off the aubergines to make stripes. Pat them dry with kitchen paper. Heat the vegetable oil in a large frying pan on a medium heat and fry the whole aubergines for 10–15 minutes, turning them occasionally until golden brown. The most important thing is to make sure that the aubergines are completely cooked all the way through; if you gently press on one of the aubergines with your finger it should be completely soft (you might need to do this in batches, adding more oil if necessary). Set aside to cool.

Add 1 tablespoon of the olive oil, the green beans and a pinch of salt to a frying pan, and sauté the beans on a high heat for 2–3 minutes or until cooked. Transfer the beans to a plate and set aside.

Add the remaining olive oil to the frying pan and cook the onions on a medium heat for about 5 minutes until soft and golden. Add the garlic and fry for a couple of minutes, then add the turmeric, cumin, black pepper, chilli powder and salt to taste, and stir for 30 seconds. Add the minced lamb and cook, using the back of a wooden spoon to crumble the meat until it browns and is fully cooked.

Add the tomato purée and stir to mix fully; add the lime juice and fry for a couple of minutes. Turn the heat off and add the green beans, chopped tomato, coriander and tarragon, mix well, then set aside.

→

Preheat the oven to 180°C/ 160°C fan/Gas 4 and line a baking tray with foil.

Using a sharp knife, make a shallow lengthways slit in each aubergine, taking care not to cut through the stalk or crown. Using your fingers, open the slits in the aubergine to form a bowl shape, leaving about 1.5cm around the edges and being careful you don't make a hole in the aubergine; if you can see big seeds, remove them. Sprinkle some salt inside the aubergine and then generously stuff each one with the meat mixture. Place on the lined baking tray and bake for 20–25 minutes. Sprinkle some flaked almonds on top, if you like, and serve.

Note
An alternative approach to preparing the aubergines is to cut them in half lengthways, without removing the stalks. Fry on both sides for 8 minutes or until soft and golden brown; set aside on kitchen paper. After making the meat filling (see above), use a fork to slash the insides of each aubergine half, leaving about 1cm around the edges. Then fill each aubergine half generously with the meat mixture.

BEEF KEBABS WITH POMEGRANATE MOLASSES, WALNUTS AND HERBS
KABAB-E TORSH

SERVES 4

1kg beef fillet, cut into 3cm pieces

FOR THE MARINADE

2 large onions, peeled and quartered
100g shelled walnuts
25g fresh flat-leaf parsley leaves
15g fresh mint leaves
3 garlic cloves
2 tbsp extra-virgin olive oil
80ml pomegranate molasses
30ml fresh lime juice
½ tsp freshly ground black pepper
1 tsp salt

This originated in northern Iran. The sourness of pomegranate molasses, the juice of the onions and the walnuts, fresh herbs and garlic combine to give the beef a tender texture and a sour flavour. Like most Iranian kebabs, this dish goes really well with rice and grilled tomatoes and with a glass of *doogh* (page 233) on the side. You can top off this dish with a pinch of sumac.

To make the marinade, blitz the onions in a food processor to create a smooth purée (adding up to 1 tablespoon of water if necessary) and then strain through a fine-mesh sieve. Discard the solids and reserve the onion juice in a large bowl. Grind the walnuts in a food processor until paste-like, then add to the bowl of onion juice. Finely chop the parsley, mint and garlic in the food processor and add to the bowl of walnuts, along with the olive oil, pomegranate molasses, lime juice, black pepper and salt. Mix well.

Add the meat to the marinade and stir well; make sure the meat is fully coated in the marinade, then cover and place in the fridge for 12 to 48 hours.

Remove excess marinade from the meat pieces and thread onto four to eight metal skewers, depending on the size of your skewers, leaving about 5cm space at the end.

For best results, cook the kebabs on a hot charcoal grill. Alternatively, cook the meat (no need to thread onto skewers) on a lightly oiled griddle pan on a medium to high heat for 2–4 minutes on each side, depending on how rare you like your meat. Serve immediately.

PERSIAN STEAK

SERVES 4

4 fillet steaks, or any other favourite steak

4 tbsp vegetable oil

FOR THE MARINADE

2 large red onions, coarsely grated

60ml fresh lime juice (retain the lime skins)

2 tsp sumac

½ tbsp freshly ground black pepper

1 tsp salt

FOR THE SAUCE

250g vine tomatoes, finely chopped

1 small red onion, finely chopped

50ml fresh lime juice

15g fresh dill leaves, finely chopped

3 tbsp olive oil

2 tsp sumac

In Iranian cuisine, meat is often marinated before grilling or roasting. In this recipe, steak is marinated overnight with onion, lime juice and black pepper, which gives the meat a tangy, peppery taste and makes it more tender and much juicier.

In a large bowl, mix all the marinade ingredients including the lime skins (chop the skins once you have juiced the limes). Add the steak to the marinade and mix well. Make sure that the meat is completely coated, then cover and place in the fridge for 12 to 48 hours.

Remove the steak from the fridge an hour before cooking so that it is at room temperature when you cook it.

Meanwhile, to make the sauce, put all the ingredients in a bowl and mix well. Season to taste and set aside.

To cook the steak, heat 2 tablespoons of the oil in a griddle pan or heavy-based frying pan on a medium to high heat until the pan is very hot. Remove excess marinade and place the meat on the pan. Do not fry more than two steaks at a time (if you do the temperature will drop and the steak will stew, rather than fry), and keep them spaced apart. Cook the steaks until they are deep brown and crisp on the outside, then turn and cook the other side. Cook for about 2 minutes on each side for rare steak, 3 minutes for medium, and 4 minutes for well done (the thickness of the steak also determine the cooking time). Pressing the steak down with a spatula will help to create a nice brown crust. If the steaks have a fatty edge, use tongs to hold the fat side down on the pan and cook for 10–20 seconds until the fat begins to run onto the pan.

Put the steaks aside for about 3 minutes before serving. This will allow the juices that have been drawn to the surface of the steak to relax back into the meat and make it more tender. Serve the steaks with the sauce on the side.

CHICKEN KEBABS WITH YOGHURT, LIME AND SAFFRON

JOOJEH KABAB

SERVES 4

1kg chicken breast fillets and boneless thighs and wings, cut into 3cm pieces

FOR THE MARINADE

2–3 generous pinches of saffron threads

¼ tsp ground turmeric

¼ tsp freshly ground black pepper

50ml fresh lime juice (retain the lime skins)

2 onions, coarsely grated

40g melted unsalted butter, cooled

100g full-fat natural yoghurt

1 tsp salt

Joojeh kabab is one of the most popular kebabs in Iran. I like to make this with a mix of chicken breasts, thighs and wings, but if you prefer you can use solely chicken breast. I recommend that you grill some tomatoes with the chicken and serve with Persian rice (pages 112–113) or with flat bread on the side.

Make the saffron water (see page 15) and set aside.

Mix all the marinade ingredients including the lime skins (chop the skins once you have juiced the limes) in a large bowl.

Add the chicken to the marinade and mix well. Cover and place in the fridge for 2 to 24 hours (the longer the better).

The traditional way to cook *joojeh kabab* is on a charcoal barbecue. Remove excess marinade from the chicken pieces and thread onto four to eight metal skewers, depending on the size of your skewers, leaving about 5cm space at the end. Place the skewers on a hot charcoal grill and cook, turning occasionally, until the chicken is charred and thoroughly cooked.

Alternatively, you can cook the chicken in the oven on the highest setting: place the chicken pieces on a lined baking tray in a single layer (no need to skewer the chicken) and cook for 15–20 minutes or until the edges of the chicken are chargrilled but the meat remains moist and juicy in the middle.

Or you can grill the chicken pieces on a lightly oiled griddle pan on a medium to high heat for 2–4 minutes on each side, until the chicken is just cooked through.

SPICY CHICKEN WITH FRIED MUSHROOMS AND LIME

STEAK-E MORGH BA GHARCH

SERVES 4

4 chicken breast fillets
5 tbsp olive oil
300g small button mushrooms
30ml fresh lime juice
20g fresh coriander or flat-leaf parsley leaves, finely chopped, to garnish

FOR THE MARINADE

2 large onions, coarsely grated
20ml fresh lime juice
½ tbsp ground turmeric
½ tsp ground cumin
¼ tsp ground cinnamon
¼ tsp freshly ground black pepper
½ tsp salt

In Iran, people use a wide range of spices to add flavour to meats, including chicken. Turmeric is one of the most widely used and I have included it in this recipe. You can serve this chicken with most of the recipes in the rice chapter of this book; alternatively, serve it with mashed potato, roasted vegetables or with salad on the side.

Put the chicken breasts on a chopping board. Placing your hand flat on top of one chicken breast, use a sharp knife to slice into one side of the breast, starting at the thicker end and cutting towards the thin point, taking care not to cut all the way through. Open out the breast so that it resembles the shape of a butterfly. Cover with cling film and pummel with a rolling pin to an even thickness. Repeat for all the chicken breasts, then set aside.

Place all the marinade ingredients in a large bowl and mix well.

Add the chicken to the bowl and, using your hand, rub the marinade all around the chicken breasts until they are fully coated in the marinade. Cover the bowl with cling film and set aside for 30 minutes or place in the fridge for up to 24 hours. Remove the chicken from the fridge an hour before cooking.

To fry the chicken, heat the oil in a large frying pan on a medium heat. Remove excess marinade from the chicken and fry on one side for 2–4 minutes or until golden. Flip the chicken breasts, add the mushrooms to the pan, and fry the other side of the chicken for 2–4 minutes or until golden. Stir the mushrooms to absorb the chicken juices. Sprinkle the lime juice over the chicken and mushrooms and fry until the juice has evaporated. (If the frying pan is not big enough, transfer the cooked chicken breasts to a large plate and cover with foil to keep warm while you fry the mushrooms in the oil.) Serve the mushrooms alongside the chicken, with a sprinkle of chopped coriander or parsley on top.

PRAWNS WITH CARAMELIZED ONION, POTATOES AND SAFFRON

DO PIAZE MEIGU

SERVES 4

2 generous pinches of saffron threads

Pinch of granulated or demerara sugar

700g baby new potatoes

Salt

6 tbsp olive oil

2 large red onions, cut in half and then finely sliced into half-moon shapes

½ tsp ground turmeric

¼ tsp chilli powder

250g mushrooms, finely sliced

450g raw peeled prawns

Fresh coriander, chopped, to garnish

This recipe, which is originally from the south of Iran, is easy to make and very tasty. The sweetness of caramelized red onion combined with potato, mushrooms, prawns and saffron water creates a beautiful flavour, which always reminds me of my grandma's kitchen. *Do piaze meigu* is usually served with a salad.

Make the saffron water (see page 15) and set aside.

Put the potatoes in a pan, add 1 teaspoon of salt and cold water to cover and bring to the boil, then simmer until they are cooked through (do not overcook). Drain and set aside to cool and then chop into 2cm pieces.

Meanwhile, add the olive oil and the onions to a large frying pan (about 30cm in diameter) on a medium heat and stir to coat the onions in the oil. Fry for 10 minutes or until the onions are soft and the edges start to turn golden brown. Stir occasionally at first and more frequently as the onions begin to change colour. Add the turmeric and chilli powder and stir for 20 seconds.

Add the mushrooms and stir for 3 minutes. Increase the heat to medium to high, add the potatoes and fry for about 4 minutes.

Add the prawns, stirring occasionally until they are almost cooked. Add 2 more tablespoons of water to the saffron water and then pour over the prawns and potatoes. Stir to mix and continue to cook until the prawns turn pink and are fully cooked and the saffron water has evaporated. Add salt to taste, transfer to a dish, garnish with coriander and serve.

GRILLED SALMON WITH DILL, BROAD BEANS AND LIME

SERVES 4

200g podded baby broad beans (fresh or frozen)

Salt

40g fresh dill leaves

4 skinless salmon fillets

20g butter

40ml fresh lime juice

Freshly ground black pepper

Although this is not an authentic Persian recipe it is inspired by the cuisine of the northern region of Iran by the Caspian Sea, which, not surprisingly, includes a lot of fish. This fish can be served with Persian rice (see pages 112–113), Barbary bread (see page 201) or mashed potato.

Place the broad beans, ¼ teaspoon of salt and 500ml of boiling water in a saucepan, bring to the boil and cook for 3–4 minutes or until the beans float in the water and are tender (cooking time will depend on the size and tenderness of the beans). Drain the beans in a colander and rinse under cold running water until cool to prevent the beans from cooking further. Squeeze the beans out of their skins and set aside.

Preheat the oven to 200°C/180°C fan/Gas 6.

Cut four pieces of foil into roughly 25 x 25cm squares.

Take a quarter of the dill and place half of it in the centre of one of the pieces of foil. Place one piece of salmon on top of the dill and then add the remaining dill on top of the salmon.

Place a couple of small knobs of butter on top of the dill and drizzle a quarter of the lime juice on top. Sprinkle a quarter of the broad beans on top and around the salmon. Add some salt and black pepper. Wrap the foil around the fish to make a parcel and place on a baking tray. Repeat this process with the three remaining salmon fillets.

Bake for 15–20 minutes (depending on the size of the salmon fillet) and serve hot.

STUFFED SEA BASS WITH CORIANDER, GARLIC AND TAMARIND

MAHI SHEKAM POR

SERVES 4

200g fresh coriander
6 tbsp vegetable or light olive oil
½ tbsp dried fenugreek (see page 12)
8 large garlic cloves, crushed
2 tsp ground turmeric, plus extra for dusting
¼–½ tsp chilli powder
Pinch of freshly ground black pepper
4 tbsp tamarind paste
Salt
4 small sea bass, gutted and de-scaled

This recipe is from the south of Iran, close to the Persian Gulf, where you can buy a wide variety of fish. The stuffing is made from fresh herbs, garlic, turmeric and tamarind, all of which are typical of recipes from southern Iran. It goes well with Persian rice (pages 112–113) or *sabzi polow* (page 117). I like to make the stuffing a little spicy, but add chilli powder to suit your taste.

Finely chop the coriander, ideally in a food processor. Place the coriander and 3 tablespoons of the oil in a non-stick frying pan on a medium heat and fry, stirring frequently, for 5–7 minutes or until the colour has changed to dark green. Add the fenugreek and stir for a minute, then set aside.

Heat the remaining oil in a saucepan on a low heat, add the garlic and cook for a couple of minutes or until it is golden but not brown, stirring constantly (do not let the garlic burn or it will make the stuffing bitter). Add the turmeric and stir for about 20 seconds. Then add the fried coriander, chilli powder to taste, black pepper, tamarind paste and 1 tablespoon of water. Turn the heat to the lowest setting and cook for a couple of minutes, then add salt to taste. Set aside to cool completely.

Preheat the oven to 200°C/180°C fan/Gas 6 and line a baking tray with baking parchment.

Rinse the fish with cold water inside and out, then pat dry. Rub some turmeric all over the fish and make three or four slashes across the flesh of each fish. Open the belly cavity of the fish and stuff each one with a quarter of the coriander stuffing. Place the fish on the lined baking tray and then tightly cover the tray with foil. Bake for 30 minutes and then remove the foil and cook for a further 7–10 minutes. Serve immediately, one fish per person.

Tip
Alternatively, you can use two medium sea bass; cook for about 45 minutes before taking the foil off.

PAN-FRIED SEA BASS WITH SPICES AND SEVILLE ORANGE JUICE

MAHI SORKH SHODEH

SERVES 4

2 tsp ground turmeric
½ tsp ground cumin
2 tsp garlic powder
¼ tsp chilli powder
Salt
4 sea bass fillets
3 tbsp vegetable or light olive oil
1–2 fresh Seville oranges or limes, cut in half

This fried fish recipe, which originated in the south of Iran, is often eaten with *sabzi polow* (page 117), especially around Persian New Year. I remember visiting my grandmother's house in Shiraz as a child and walking with her to the garden to pick some Seville oranges from the trees to make this dish. Seville oranges are not in season all year round (find them between the end of December and mid-February), but you can substitute the Seville orange with lime. I like to use sea bass but you can use any fish fillets.

In a small bowl, mix the turmeric, cumin, garlic powder, chilli and a good pinch of salt. Set aside.

Pat the sea bass fillets dry with kitchen paper and place on a tray (if the fillets are thick, score the skin five or six times at approximately 1cm intervals).

Sprinkle the spice mixture over the fish and spread it with your hand before flipping the fish fillets over and doing the same on the other side. Set aside.

To cook the fish, heat the oil in a frying pan until hot. Place the fillets, skin-side down, in the pan. Cook until the skin is golden and crisp and the flesh begins to change colour.

Turn the fillets over and cook for 1–3 minutes (depending on the thickness of the fillet). Squeeze some fresh Seville orange or lime juice over the fillets and fry for a further minute or so until all the liquid is evaporated. Serve immediately.

"If it is bread that you seek, you will have bread.
If it is the soul you seek, you will find the soul.
If you understand this secret,
You know you are that which you seek."

Rumi

Sangak Bread, Isfahan, Iran (April 2017)

BREAD, PIZZA & PASTA

BARBARY BREAD

MAKES 2

1 tsp sugar

1 tsp salt

50ml extra-virgin olive oil

250g strong white bread flour

1 x 7g sachet or 2 tsp fast-action dried yeast

2 tbsp dried chives

2 tbsp hemp seeds (optional)

Semolina flour for dusting

FOR THE GLAZE

1 tbsp plain flour

1 tbsp olive oil

150ml water

Small pinch of salt

FOR THE TOPPING

(*choose one or use a mixture*)

Sesame seeds

Nigella seeds

Sunflower seeds

Barbary bread is one of Iran's best-known types of bread. It is crunchy on the outside and soft and fluffy on the inside. My recipe is a variation on the traditional version, and can be served with most starters and salads, or as a snack on its own.

In a large bowl, mix the sugar, salt and olive oil with 50ml cold water mixed with 100ml boiling water. Add half of the flour and stir until smooth, using a wooden spoon. Add the yeast and stir to mix, then add the remaining flour and mix again. Transfer to a stand mixer and knead, using the dough hook, for about 8 minutes. Add the chives and hemp seeds, if using, and knead until completely mixed. Cover the bowl with cling film and leave to rest for 15 minutes.

Alternatively, knead the dough by hand on a lightly floured work surface for 10–15 minutes or until smooth and elastic. Place the dough in a bowl, cover with cling film and leave to rest for 15 minutes.

Lightly sprinkle some semolina flour over a large baking tray and set aside.

Tip the dough onto a lightly floured surface and divide into two equal parts. Working with one half of the dough, shape it into a long log (about 25cm) and, using your fingers, form into an oval shape approximately 30 x 9cm. Transfer the dough to the baking tray and then, using your fingers, make two lengthways grooves in the dough. Repeat this process for the other half of the dough. Cover the baking tray with cling film and leave to prove for 1 hour.

Preheat the oven to 220°C/200°C fan/Gas 7.

While the dough is rising, prepare the glaze: combine all the ingredients in a small saucepan and bring to the boil on a medium heat, stirring constantly. Boil for a minute (at this point it should have the consistency of a thin béchamel), then remove from the heat and set aside.

When the dough has risen, very gently brush a thin layer of glaze over it without pressing down on the dough (discard any leftover glaze) and sprinkle your favourite seeds on top. Bake in the centre of the oven for 12–15 minutes or until the top is golden. Leave to cool before slicing.

PIZZA WITH PERSIAN PESTO, CHARGRILLED AUBERGINE AND MOZZARELLA

MAKES 4

200g strong white bread flour

200g 00 flour

100g semolina flour, plus extra for dusting

1 x 7g sachet or 2 tsp of fast-action dried yeast

2 tsp sugar

1 tsp salt

FOR THE TOPPING

4 garlic cloves, crushed

5 tbsp extra-virgin olive oil

3 large aubergines, cut into 1cm discs

55g shelled pistachios

55g shelled walnuts

40g fresh mint leaves

40g fresh flat-leaf parsley leaves

40g fresh coriander

400g feta cheese, finely crumbled

4 x 125g mozzarella balls, sliced

2 red onions, sliced into rings

3 tbsp sesame seeds

Although not a traditional Iranian food, pizza is extremely popular in Iran. This pizza is inspired by Persian ingredients and is very popular with friends who visit my home in London.

In the bowl of a stand mixer, add all the dough ingredients, plus 100ml cold water mixed with 250ml boiling water. Using the dough hook, knead for about 8 minutes until the dough forms a ball. Alternatively, mix the ingredients with a wooden spoon before placing the dough on a lightly floured work surface and kneading for 10–15 minutes or until the dough is smooth and elastic. Shape the dough into a ball.

Place the dough in a bowl, cover with cling film and leave to rest for 1 hour.

Meanwhile, make the topping. Preheat a griddle pan on a medium heat. In a small bowl, mix the garlic and the olive oil. Generously brush both sides of the aubergine discs with the garlicky oil (add more olive oil if needed), sprinkle with salt and chargrill for 4–6 minutes. Set aside. Reserve the garlic cloves.

Finely grind the pistachios and walnuts in a food processor. Transfer them to a large bowl.

Finely chop the mint, parsley and coriander in the food processor and add them to the bowl of ground nuts. Add the feta cheese and the reserved garlic, mix well and set aside.

Preheat the oven to 220°C/200°C fan/Gas 7.

Divide the dough into four balls. Scatter some semolina flour on your work surface and roll out the dough to make four thin pizza bases (about 2mm thick). Sprinkle two baking sheets with semolina flour and place the pizza bases on them. Depending on how many you can fit on the baking sheets, you may need to do this in batches.

Crumble the feta, nut and herb mixture evenly over the four pizza bases. Then add the chargrilled aubergine, mozzarella and onions and sprinkle with sesame seeds. Bake for 15–17 minutes or until the bases are crisp and golden brown around the edges and the cheese has melted.

PERSIAN MINI PIZZA

MAKES 8

200g strong white bread flour

200g 00 flour

100g semolina flour, plus extra for dusting

1 x 7g sachet or 2 tsp of fast-action dried yeast

2 tsp sugar

1 tsp salt

Extra-virgin olive oil

FOR THE TOPPING

120g minced lamb (up to 20% fat)

1 red onion, coarsely grated

1 tsp ground turmeric

1 tsp ground cumin

½ tsp ground cinnamon

½ tsp freshly ground black pepper

Pinch of chilli powder

Salt

70g good-quality tomato purée

60ml fresh lime juice

300g mushrooms, finely sliced

100g cheddar cheese, coarsely grated

1 x 125g mozzarella ball, coarsely grated

2 small vine tomatoes (about 150g), coarsely grated

1 small green pepper, chopped into 1cm cubes

60g tinned sweetcorn, drained

Although I tasted pizza when I lived in Italy as a child, I first encountered a mini pizza in Tehran: it was a nice surprise because I can never finish a full pizza. Although not a Persian dish, pizza has become one of the most popular foods in Iran, especially with the younger generation. In all the major cities and towns, you can find busy restaurants and pizzerias that would not be out of place in Napoli or New York. Iranian pizza, also known as Persian pizza, uses much the same toppings as Italian pizza. However, what differentiates Iranian pizza is the taste, which is derived from the spices used in the toppings. In other words, the difference is in the preparation of the ingredients rather than the kind of toppings used. This pizza features an interesting combination of ingredients, including minced lamb, lime juice and spices. The method used to make the pizza base results in a thick bread base that is soft and fluffy inside but quite crunchy on the outside.

In the bowl of a stand mixer, add all the flour, yeast, sugar and salt to 100ml cold water mixed with 250ml boiling water. Using the dough hook, knead for about 8 minutes until the dough forms a ball. Alternatively, mix the ingredients with a wooden spoon before placing the dough on a lightly floured work surface and kneading for 10–15 minutes or until the dough is smooth and elastic. Shape the dough into a ball.

Add 5 tablespoons of olive oil to a large bowl and place the dough in the bowl, cover with cling film and leave to rest for 15 minutes.

Flip the bowl to tip the dough onto your work surface. Very gently, and without reshaping the dough ball, divide it into eight equal pieces. Take one of the dough pieces and, using your fingers, flatten it into a circle (approximately 15cm in diameter) on a large baking tray. Repeat this

→

process until you have used all the dough (you should have two baking trays with four pieces of pizza dough on each). Cover the baking trays with cling film and leave the dough to prove for 1 hour, until risen.

Meanwhile, make the topping. Using your hands, mix the meat, onion, turmeric, cumin, cinnamon, black pepper, chilli powder and a pinch of salt in a bowl. Add to a frying pan with 2 tablespoons of olive oil on a medium heat, breaking up the meat using the back of a wooden spoon, and fry until the meat is browned and fully cooked. Add 30g of the tomato purée and stir to mix fully before adding the lime juice and stir to mix, until the lime juice has fully evaporated. Set aside.

In a large saucepan, add the mushrooms, 4 tablespoons of olive oil and a pinch of salt, and stir on a high heat for 2–3 minutes or until the mushrooms are almost cooked. Set aside.

In a bowl, mix the cheddar and mozzarella cheeses together and set aside.

Preheat the oven to 220°C/ 200°C fan/Gas 7.

To assemble the pizza, mix the grated tomatoes, the remaining tomato purée and a pinch of salt in a small bowl. Divide the mix evenly across the pizza dough circles: do this gently and avoid pressing down on the dough to prevent the air, which is created in the dough base, from being released. Sprinkle some cheese on top followed by some mushrooms, meat, green pepper and sweetcorn. Don't be concerned if your pizzas appear to be overloaded with ingredients, because these will shrink as they cook. Bake for 16–18 minutes or until the edges are golden.

PERSIAN MACARONI

SERVES 4

230g minced lamb (up to 20% fat)
1 large red onion, coarsely grated
1½ tsp ground turmeric
1 tsp ground cumin
½ tsp ground cinnamon
½ tsp freshly ground black pepper
¼ tsp chilli powder
Salt
Olive oil
2 tbsp cumin seeds
180g good-quality tomato purée
300g mushrooms, finely sliced
100g petits pois (fresh or frozen)
1 green pepper, chopped into 1cm cubes
80ml fresh lime juice
350g dried spaghetti, broken into three roughly equal pieces
Knob of butter
1–2 potatoes, peeled and sliced approx. 5mm thick

This is quite different from Italian-style pasta dishes because of the cooking method, which is similar to the steaming method used to cook Persian rice. This recipe includes a crispy base, which is called *tahdig* and is one of the finest delicacies in Persian cuisine. I have used potatoes, but you could also make a *flatbread tahdig* (see page 113). In Iran, this is often served with a drizzle of chilli sauce.

Using your hands, mix the meat, onion, turmeric, cumin, cinnamon, black pepper, chilli and a pinch of salt in a bowl. Heat 5 tablespoons of olive oil in a large frying pan on a medium heat, add the meat mixture, breaking up the meat using the back of a wooden spoon, and fry until the meat is browned. Add the cumin seeds and tomato purée, mix well and fry for a couple of minutes. Add the mushrooms, peas and green pepper, stir and then add the lime juice, mix well and fry for a couple of minutes. Taste and adjust the seasoning if needed. Set aside.

Half fill a large non-stick pan (about 25cm in diameter, with a snug-fitting lid) with water and add 2 tablespoons of oil and 1 tablespoon of salt. Bring to the boil, add the pasta, give it a good stir, and cook according to the packet instructions, until fully cooked and still slightly al dente. Drain and set aside in a colander.

Heat 3 tablespoons of olive oil and a knob of butter in the pan that the pasta was cooked in and add a single layer of sliced potatoes.

Add a layer of pasta on top of the potatoes, followed by a layer of meat sauce. Repeat this process until all the pasta is used up. Place the lid on the pan tightly (see step 6 on page 113). Place the pan on a high heat for 5 minutes (this will allow steam to build up inside the pan). Then reduce the heat to the lowest setting and cook for 1 hour.

To serve, gently mix the layers of pasta and meat sauce and then spoon out the pasta onto a serving dish until you expose the crispy *tahdig* at the bottom of the pan. Serve the *tahdig* on a separate plate.

PASTA WITH SMOKED AUBERGINE, FETA AND MINT

MACARONI-E BADEMJAN

SERVES 4

3 large aubergines, smoked (see page 12)

4 large onions

Vegetable oil for frying

8 tbsp extra-virgin olive oil

Salt

300g dried pasta, such as penne

1 large bulb of garlic, cloves separated and crushed

1 tsp ground turmeric

½ tsp ground cumin

70g good-quality tomato purée

250g fresh shiitake mushrooms, finely sliced

50ml fresh lime juice

20g fresh mint leaves, finely chopped, plus extra to garnish

200–250g feta cheese, crumbled

Aubergine is one of my favourite vegetables, especially when it is smoked, which gives the flesh a strong and interesting flavour. This is not a traditional Persian dish but it is inspired by Persian cooking, combining the deep flavours of smoked aubergine with feta cheese and mint. I usually make the smoked aubergine the day before to save time.

Peel the smoked aubergines (see page 12), then mash them using the back of a fork. Set aside.

Make the crispy fried onion topping (see page 91) and set aside.

Preheat the oven to 200°C/180°C fan/Gas 6.

Half-fill a large saucepan with water, add 2 tablespoons of the olive oil and 1 tablespoon of salt and bring to the boil. Add the pasta and cook according to the packet instructions. Drain and set aside in a colander.

Meanwhile, place the garlic in a large frying pan with the remaining 6 tablespoons of olive oil. Cook on a low heat, stirring frequently, until the garlic is lightly golden. Add the turmeric and cumin and stir to mix. Add the aubergine, turn the heat to medium and cook for 4 minutes, stirring and mashing all the time. Add the tomato purée and cook for a further couple of minutes, stirring constantly.

Add the mushrooms and stir for a couple of minutes before adding the lime juice. Stir until all the liquid has evaporated, season to taste and turn off the heat. Add the mint and the drained pasta and stir to mix.

Spoon half of the pasta mixture into a large baking dish. Level the surface and then add half of the crumbled feta followed by two-thirds of the reserved crispy fried onion. Add the remaining pasta in an even layer and then sprinkle the remaining cheese on top.

Bake in the centre of the oven for 20 minutes or until the cheese on top is golden. Sprinkle the rest of the crispy fried onion and the chopped mint on top and serve.

DESSERTS & DRINKS

SAFFRON ICE CREAM AND CARROT JUICE
HAVIJ BASTANI

MAKES 8-10 GLASSES

100g good-quality white chocolate with vanilla

3-4 generous pinches of saffron threads

Pinch of granulated or demerara sugar

300ml full-fat milk

300ml double cream

100g condensed milk

Freshly made carrot juice

Crushed pistachios for topping

It may seem strange to mix ice cream and juice but most ice cream shops in Iran serve saffron ice cream with carrot juice and many of my European friends who have visited Iran have become addicted to it. Of course, you can eat the saffron ice cream on its own but I would encourage you to add carrot juice if you are feeling adventurous.

Break the chocolate into a large heatproof bowl and set aside.

Make saffron water (see page 15) and add it to a saucepan along with the milk, cream and condensed milk. Bring to the boil on a medium heat, stirring every now and then. Reduce the heat to low and simmer for 5 minutes, then pour into the bowl of chocolate. Stir until the chocolate has completely melted and then set aside to cool before placing in the fridge to chill.

Pour the chilled mixture into an ice-cream machine and churn according to the manufacturer's instructions. Alternatively, if you don't have an ice-cream machine, whisk the chilled mixture for 5 minutes on high speed, then freeze for 4 to 5 hours, stirring every hour until almost frozen.

Freeze the ice cream for a couple of hours so that it is hard before serving.

To make *havij bastani*, place two or three scoops of ice cream in a glass and then pour in some carrot juice to fill the glass. Top with some crushed pistachios and serve.

RICE AND ALMOND PUDDING
FERENI

SERVES 4

6 cardamom pods
700ml milk (preferably full-fat)
40g rice flour
1 tbsp rose water
60g ground almonds
4 tbsp honey

TO GARNISH

Your favourite berries or fruits, such as sliced banana, apple, peach or persimmon
Crushed pistachios
Ground cinnamon

As a teenager growing up in Isfahan, I have fond memories of going out with friends to have *fereni*. This creamy aromatic pudding is extremely popular throughout Iran; some people even eat it for breakfast. It is usually served with various kinds of syrups, such as grape syrup, date syrup, or maple syrup. You can also serve it with *sharbat-e shahtoot* (page 235).

Crack the cardamom pods in a mortar with a pestle to release the seeds. Discard the pods and grind the seeds to a fine powder. Add the ground cardamom to a saucepan along with the milk, rice flour, rose water, ground almonds and honey.

Stir with a balloon whisk until all the ingredients are fully mixed. Bring to the boil on a medium heat, stirring frequently. As soon as it starts to boil, turn down the heat and simmer for 20 seconds (at this point the consistency should be like a béchamel sauce).

Divide between four serving bowls and leave to cool, then place the bowls in the fridge to chill for at least an hour. (It can be made a day ahead, but it's much nicer eaten on the same day.)

To serve, garnish with your choice of fruit, a sprinkling of crushed pistachios and a dusting of cinnamon on top.

WALNUT, PISTACHIO AND ALMOND MUFFINS

MAKES 12

120g plain flour

1½ tsp baking powder

Salt

220g unsalted butter, at room temperature

150g caster sugar

½ tbsp vanilla extract

1 tbsp rose water

8–12 cardamom pods (depending on the size of the cardamom seeds), seeds removed and ground to a fine powder

4 eggs, at room temperature

100g sour cream

100g ground almonds

100g shelled walnuts, roughly chopped

60g shelled pistachios, roughly chopped

100g flaked almonds

These buttery muffins are a wonderful treat with tea. I have included walnuts, pistachios and almonds because I like the texture as well as the combination of flavours. In Iran, yoghurt is often used in cakes but I like to use sour cream. If you prefer, you can make this as a cake in a 20cm cake tin; if you do, then increase the baking time to 1 hour 10 minutes.

Preheat the oven to 160°C/140°C fan/Gas 3. Line a 12-hole cupcake tin with paper cases.

Sift the flour, baking powder and a pinch of salt into a bowl and set aside.

Using an electric mixer, beat the butter and sugar together, first on a low speed and then on a high speed until very pale and fluffy, which will take about 10 minutes (halfway through, scrape down the sides of bowl using a rubber spatula). When done, scrape down the sides of the bowl again and then add the vanilla, rose water and ground cardamom. Beat for a couple of minutes on a medium speed before adding the eggs, one at a time, beating and scraping the bowl thoroughly after you add each egg.

Add the flour, sour cream and ground almonds and beat until fully incorporated. Add the walnuts and pistachios and mix with a large spoon until evenly combined.

Divide the batter equally between the muffin cases. Then, press down the batter into each case gently to ensure that they are even. Sprinkle generously with flaked almonds and gently press down.

Bake for 35–40 minutes or until golden brown on top. If you insert a skewer into the centre of one of the muffins it should come out clean. Leave to cool before eating. The muffins can be kept in an airtight container for up to 4 days.

CRUNCHY WALNUT PUFFS

NOON-E GERDUI

MAKES ABOUT 100 TINY PUFFS

150g shelled walnuts

1 vanilla pod

3 egg yolks

3 tbsp caster sugar

¼–½ tsp vanilla extract (if you are not using a vanilla pod you will need ½ tsp)

This crunchy sweet, which is especially popular during Iranian New Year, goes really well with black tea. When I eat these, my mind wanders back to New Year celebrations in Iran and how exciting it was to watch my mother make these sweets in our kitchen. You can make these walnut puffs in different sizes but they are usually made quite small.

Coarsely chop the walnuts, taking care not to chop them too finely as you need to retain their crunchy texture. Set aside.

Slit the vanilla pod lengthways using a sharp knife and scrape out the tiny black seeds. Place the egg yolks, sugar, vanilla extract and vanilla seeds in a bowl and whisk, using an electric mixer, until the mixture is firm, pale yellow, has tripled in volume and falls in thick ribbons when you lift the beaters; this should take about 10–12 minutes.

Add the chopped walnuts to the egg mixture and fold in evenly, using a rubber spatula.

Preheat the oven to 160°C/140°C fan/Gas 3 and line a baking sheet with baking parchment.

Taking 1 teaspoon of the mixture at a time, place on the baking paper, leaving a 2cm gap between the walnut puffs (they should be no bigger than a hazelnut).

Bake for 18–20 minutes. When you remove them from the oven, the walnut puffs should be easy to separate from the baking paper and should have a crunchy texture. Leave the walnut puffs to cool on the baking sheet. Store in an airtight jar for up to 4 days.

DATES WITH CRUNCHY WALNUTS AND BUTTERY CREAM

RANGINAK

SERVES 6-8

25 Persian dates, or Medjool dates
80g shelled walnuts
40g plain flour
40g unsalted butter, at room temperature
½ tsp olive oil
¼–½ tsp ground cinnamon
Flaked or halved almonds to garnish
Roughly chopped pistachios to garnish

This delicious dessert is from the south of Iran but it is popular throughout the country. It is usually served with black tea. If possible, use Persian dates, which are available in most Middle Eastern stores. If you can't find Persian dates then use Medjool dates; these are larger than Persian dates so you might want to add more walnuts.

Split the dates along the middle, leaving one side attached; discard the stones. Generously fill the dates with walnuts (at least half a walnut to each date, or more if you are using Medjool dates). Close the dates so that the walnuts are fully enclosed.

Place the stuffed dates upright on a small plate, packing them tightly in a circular shape.

To make the buttery cream, sprinkle the flour in a frying pan on a medium heat and stir constantly with a wooden spoon for 3–5 minutes. The colour of the flour should change to light beige. Remove the pan from the heat and add the butter and olive oil, stirring until it is completely mixed with the flour to create a sauce. Before it cools, spoon it evenly over the dates.

Dust the cinnamon over the buttery cream and sprinkle the flaked almonds and chopped pistachios on top.

FLOWER BAKLAVA WITH STICKY SYRUP
BAGHLAVA GOL

MAKES 30

90g shelled pistachios
55g shelled walnuts
55g ground almonds
½ tbsp caster sugar
¼ tsp ground cinnamon
4 cardamom pods, seeds removed and ground to a fine powder
6 sheets of filo pastry (approx. 50 x 30cm)
Melted unsalted butter for brushing

FOR THE SYRUP

200g caster sugar
125ml water
125ml rose water
100g honey
3 cardamom pods
1 tbsp fresh lime juice
Pinch of saffron threads

Baklava is a sweet pastry filled with chopped nuts and drenched in a sticky syrup. It is characteristic of the cuisines of the former Ottoman Empire and can be found in Turkey, Greece, Armenia and Syria, among other countries, as well as in Iran. Traditionally, baklava comprises layers of filo pastry filled with nuts, but for this version I have created a flower-shaped baklava. In Iran, this is usually served with black tea.

Preheat the oven to 200°C/180°C fan/Gas 6 and line a baking sheet with baking parchment.

Finely grind the pistachios and walnuts in a food processor and place in a large bowl along with the ground almonds, sugar, cinnamon and ground cardamom. Mix well and set aside.

Unwrap the filo pastry and keep under a damp tea towel until ready to use. Brush one sheet of filo pastry with melted butter and cut into 15 squares (each square should be approximately 10 x 10cm). Place three squares of filo on top of one another at an angle to form a star shape. Place 1 tablespoon of the nut mixture in the centre of each star, then gather up the edges of the pastry and pinch tightly together to enclose the filling and make a pastry pouch (flower). Place the pastry pouch on the lined baking sheet and brush lightly with melted butter. Repeat this process until you have created 30 flower baklavas.

Bake for 7–10 minutes or until golden. Remove from the oven and leave to cool, then place on a large dish.

To make the syrup, put all the ingredients in a saucepan on a medium to high heat, stirring frequently until the sugar has fully dissolved. Bring to the boil and then turn the heat down to medium and simmer for 12–14 minutes or until you have a thick, sticky syrup. Remove from the heat and discard the cardamom pods. Pour the piping hot syrup on top of the flower baklavas and leave to cool completely before serving.

PERSIAN DELICACY
LATIFEH

MAKES 14

40g shelled pistachios
3 large eggs, separated
90g icing sugar, plus extra for dusting
6 cardamom pods, seeds removed and ground to a fine powder
½ tbsp vanilla extract
70g self-raising flour
25g cornflour

FOR THE CREAM FILLING

300ml double cream
2 tsp icing sugar
¼ tsp rose water

This is one of my favourite sweets, which I first had in Tabriz, a city in the north-west of Iran where I studied for several years. It is called *latifeh*, which means 'delicacy' in Farsi, which makes sense because this dessert is as light as a feather. You will need a piping bag.

Preheat the oven to 220°C/200°C fan/Gas 7 and line a baking sheet with baking parchment.

Finely grind the pistachios in a food processor. Set aside.

Using an electric mixer on a medium speed, whisk the egg whites with half of the icing sugar until the mixture is glossy and stands up in stiff peaks when the beaters are lifted – do not overdo it. Add the ground pistachios and whisk for a further 30 seconds. Set aside.

Place the egg yolks in a separate bowl and add the remaining icing sugar, ground cardamom and vanilla. Using an electric mixer, whisk on a high speed until the mixture is very pale, has tripled in volume and falls in thick ribbons when you lift the beaters (be careful it does not get too thick and firm).

Gently fold the egg yolk mixture into the beaten egg whites in two batches. Do not over-fold it as you need to keep the air in the mixture. Mix the flour and cornflour in a bowl and then sift over the egg mixture in two batches and gently fold in.

Transfer the mixture to a piping bag. With the bag held vertically, pipe 4–5cm diameter circles onto the lined tin, about 2cm apart. Bake for 6–8 minutes or until the pastries are golden (check frequently as they burn easily). Set aside to cool completely.

While the pastries are cooling, prepare the filling. Place all the filling ingredients in a bowl and whisk until thick peaks form.

Once cool, sandwich the pastries together with the whipped cream and chill in the fridge for a couple of hours. To serve, dust some icing sugar on top.

MINTY YOGHURT DRINK
DOOGH

MAKES 1.2 LITRES

1 tbsp dried mint

½ tsp dried oregano

½ tsp dried thyme

1 tsp edible dried rose petals

600g natural yoghurt (preferably full-fat)

1 tsp salt

600ml chilled sparkling water

Ice cubes to serve (optional)

Crushed rose petals to garnish (optional)

This refreshing drink was popular in ancient Persia and remains popular in modern-day Iran. It is traditionally made with sour yoghurt, but that can be hard to find in the west; this recipe uses natural yoghurt and sparkling water, and is close to what I used to drink in Iran. It is perfect on a hot summer's day but people in Iran tend to drink it all year round, usually as an accompaniment to food, especially kebab.

In a spice grinder, grind all the dried herbs and petals until they are as smooth as flour.

Put the yoghurt in a large bowl, add the ground herb mixture and the salt and beat well for a couple of minutes until smooth.

Transfer the yoghurt to a large jug and gently add the sparkling water. Mix well (do not over-stir as the sparkling water will become flat), taste and add more salt if needed before adding some ice cubes (ice cubes are optional) and serve immediately. You can refrigerate the *doogh* up to 24 hours.

PERSIAN BLACKBERRY DRINK
SHARBAT-E SHAHTOOT

MAKES 8-10 GLASSES

400g caster sugar
400g blackberries
½ tsp vanilla extract
Ice cubes to serve

This blackberry drink is served throughout Iran during the summer season. For me it has a nostalgic quality: I have fond memories of my aunt making it for me as a child when I visited her in Shiraz. If kept in the fridge in a sealed bottle it will remain fresh for months. Because *sharbat-e shahtoot* has a syrupy texture you can also pour it over desserts and cakes.

Heat 750ml cold water and the sugar in a saucepan on a medium heat and stir until the water boils and the sugar has completely dissolved.

Place the blackberries in a muslin cloth and tie securely.

Place the bag of blackberries in the boiling syrup and bring back to the boil. Simmer on a low heat for 35–45 minutes or until the liquid turns into a dark syrup; the cooking time will vary, depending on the ripeness of the berries.

Add the vanilla extract and boil for a couple of minutes, then remove the pan from the heat.

Carefully remove the bag of blackberries from the syrup. Pour the syrup into a bottle and leave to cool completely. Seal the bottle and place in the fridge.

To serve, add 1 to 2 parts syrup to 4 or 5 parts water (depending on how sweet you like your drink). Stir well, add ice cubes and serve. You can store the leftover syrup in an airtight bottle in the fridge for up to 3 months.

Note
After making the syrup, you can use the blackberries to make jam: untie the muslin cloth and tip the berries into a saucepan, along with 100ml of the syrup. Bring to the boil and gently simmer for 5–7 minutes or until it thickens. Transfer to a jar and leave to cool before placing in the fridge.

Ali Qapu Palace, Naqsh-e Jahan Square, Isfahan, Iran (April 2018)

INDEX

A

almonds: barberries, pistachios and almonds in saffron with rice 119
    caramelized nuts in leaf cups 65
    flower baklava with sticky syrup 229
    rice and almond pudding 221
    walnut, pistachio and almond muffins 223
ash, toppings for 91
aubergines 12
    aubergine and okra stew 159
    aubergine and Persian *kashk* dip 37
    chargrilled aubergine and beetroot with saffron yoghurt 63
    pasta with smoked aubergine, feta and mint 211
    Persian stuffed aubergine 175–6
    pizza with Persian pesto, chargrilled aubergine and mozzarella 203
    smoked aubergine with garlic and yoghurt 29
    smoked aubergine with tomatoes, garlic and eggs 35
    yellow split peas with lamb 151–2

B

baklava with sticky syrup 229
barbary bread 201
barberries 12
    barberries, pistachios and almonds in saffron with rice 119
    chicken with orange juice and barberries 83
    Persian meatballs in tomato and herb sauce 145
    Persian potato patties 81
    prawns, barberries and saffron with rice 129
    saffron yoghurt rice cupcakes 121
beef: beef kebabs with pomegranate molasses, walnuts and herbs 179
    meat samosas 43
    Persian steak 181
    turnip soup with meatballs 93
beetroot: beetroot with spinach and creamy yoghurt 31
    chargrilled aubergine and beetroot with saffron yoghurt 63
blackberry drink, Persian 235
bread, barbary 201
broad beans: broad beans with garlic, dill and egg 75
    grilled salmon with dill, broad beans and lime 189
    rice with broad beans and dill 131
    salmon, broad bean and dill frittata 73

C

carrots: chicken with carrots, prunes and saffron 157
    Persian pearl barley soup 95
    salad olivieh 57
    saffron ice cream and carrot juice 219
cheese: caramelized onion and chickpea salad 55
    chargrilled aubergine and beetroot with saffron yoghurt 63
    cheese and potato samosas 41
    fresh herb frittata with feta cheese 77
    goat's cheese with fresh herbs and walnuts 33
    pasta with smoked aubergine, feta and mint 211
    Persian mini pizza 205–6
    pizza with Persian pesto, chargrilled aubergine and mozzarella 203
    watermelon, feta cheese and mint salad 61
    yoghurt and chickpea soup 97
chelow method, cooking rice 112
chicken: aubergine and okra stew 159
    chicken kebabs with yoghurt, lime and saffron 183
    chicken with carrots, prunes and saffron 157
    chicken with orange juice and barberries 163
    chicken with walnuts and pomegranate molasses 161
    Persian pearl barley soup 95
    saffron yoghurt rice cupcakes 121
    salad olivieh 57
    spicy chicken with fried mushrooms and lime 185
chicken livers with caramelized onion and coriander 39
chickpeas: caramelized onion and chickpea salad 55
    yoghurt and chickpea soup 97
chocolate: saffron ice cream and carrot juice 219
cod with fresh herbs, garlic and tamarind 165
cucumber: cucumber, red onion and pomegranate salad 53
    goat's cheese with fresh herbs and walnuts 33
    Persian potato salad 59
    salad olivieh 57
    Shirazi salad 51
    yoghurt with cucumber, mint and dill 27

D

dal, Persian 141
dates with crunchy walnuts and buttery cream 227
drinks: minty yoghurt drink 233
    Persian blackberry drink 235

E

eggs: broad beans with garlic, dill and egg 75
    fresh herb frittata with feta cheese 77
    Persian omelette 79
    Persian potato patties 81
    Persian potato salad 59
    salad olivieh 57
    salmon, broad bean and dill frittata 73
    smoked aubergine with tomatoes, garlic and eggs 35

F

fenugreek leaves 12
flower baklava with sticky syrup 229

frittata: fresh herb frittata with feta cheese 77
  salmon, broad bean and dill frittata 73

G
garlic: crispy fried garlic topping 91
goat's cheese with fresh herbs and walnuts 33
golpar 12–13
green beans: rice with green beans and lamb 133
  Persian stuffed aubergine 175

I
ice cream: saffron ice cream and carrot juice 219

K
kashk 13
  aubergine and Persian *kashk* dip 37
kebabs: beef kebabs with pomegranate molasses, walnuts and herbs 179
  chicken kebabs with yoghurt, lime and saffron 183
kohlrabi: herbed rice and kohlrabi with tiny meatballs 125–6

L
lamb: aubergine and okra stew 159
  herbed rice and kohlrabi with tiny meatballs 125–6
  lamb shanks with quince and prunes 155
  lamb shanks with saffron 149
  meat samosas 43
  minced meat and potato cakes 83
  pan kebab with tomato and mushroom sauce 173
  Persian macaroni 209
  Persian meatballs in tomato and herb sauce 145–6
  Persian mini pizza 205–6
  Persian stuffed aubergine 175–6
  pomegranate soup with meatballs 105
  rice with green beans and lamb 133
  slow-cooked lamb with fresh herbs and beans 143
  turnip soup with meatballs 93
  yellow split peas with lamb 151–2
lentils: lentils with rice and cumin 123
  Persian dal 141
lettuce: caramelized nuts in leaf cups 65
limes, Persian dried 13
liver *see* chicken livers

M
matchstick fries 152
meat samosas 43
meatballs: herbed rice and kohlrabi with tiny meatballs 125–6
  Persian meatballs in tomato and herb sauce 145–6
  pomegranate soup with meatballs 105
  turnip soup with meatballs 93
mint, dried 13
  fried mint topping 37, 91
muffins: walnut, pistachio and almond 223

N
noodles: Persian noodle and herb soup 101
  yoghurt and chickpea soup 97
nuts 13
  caramelized nuts in leaf cups 65
  see also almonds, pistachios, walnuts etc

O
okra: aubergine and okra stew 159
olives: marinated olives with walnuts and mint 25
omelette, Persian 79
onions: crispy fried onion topping 29, 91
oranges: chicken with orange juice and barberries 163
  pan-fried sea bass with spices and Seville orange juice 193

P
pan kebab with tomato and mushroom sauce 173
pasta: pasta with smoked aubergine, feta and mint 211
  Persian macaroni 209
pastries: cheese and potato samosas 41
  flower baklava with sticky syrup 229
  meat samosas 43
  Persian delicacy 231
pearl barley soup 95
Persian blackberry drink 235
Persian dal 141
Persian delicacy 231
Persian macaroni 209
Persian meatballs in tomato and herb sauce 145–6
Persian mini pizza 205–6
Persian noodle and herb soup 101
Persian omelette 79
Persian pearl barley soup 95
Persian potato patties 81
Persian potato salad 59
Persian steak 181
Persian stuffed aubergine 175–6
Persian tomato soup 103
pinto beans: hot bean soup 99
pistachios: barberries, pistachios and almonds in saffron with rice 119
  flower baklava with sticky syrup 229
  Persian delicacy 231
  walnut, pistachio and almond muffins 223
pizza: Persian mini pizza 205–6
  pizza with Persian pesto, chargrilled aubergine and mozzarella 203
pomegranate molasses 15
  beef kebabs with pomegranate molasses, walnuts and herbs 179
  chicken with carrots, prunes and saffron 157
  chicken with walnuts and pomegranate molasses 161
  marinated olives with walnuts and mint 25
  pomegranate soup with meatballs 105
pomegranates 13–15

chargrilled aubergine and beetroot with saffron yoghurt 63
cucumber, red onion and pomegranate salad 53
marinated olives with walnuts and mint 25
pomegranate soup with meatballs 105
watermelon, feta cheese and mint salad 61
potatoes: cheese and potato samosas 41
matchstick fries 152
minced meat and potato cakes 83
Persian potato patties 81
Persian potato salad 59
prawns with caramelized onion, potatoes and saffron 187
salad olivieh 57
prawns: prawns, barberries and saffron with rice 129
prawns with caramelized onion, potatoes and saffron 187
prunes 12
chicken with carrots, prunes and saffron 157
lamb shanks with quince and prunes 155

Q
quinces: lamb shanks with quince and prunes 155

R
red kidney beans: slow-cooked lamb with fresh herbs and beans 143
reshteh 15
Persian noodle and herb soup 101
yoghurt and chickpea soup 97
rice 13, 112–15, 126
barberries, pistachios and almonds in saffron with rice 119
herbed rice and kohlrabi with tiny meatballs 125–6
lentils with rice and cumin 123
prawns, barberries and saffron with rice 129
rice and almond pudding 221

rice with broad beans and dill 131
rice with fresh herbs 117
rice with green beans and lamb 133
saffron yoghurt rice cupcakes 121
rose water 15

S
saffron 15
chicken with carrots, prunes and saffron 157
saffron ice cream and carrot juice 219
lamb shanks with saffron 149
prawns, barberries and saffron with rice 129
saffron water 15
saffron yoghurt rice cakes 121
salmon: grilled salmon with dill, broad beans and lime 189
salmon, broad bean and dill frittata 73
samosas: cheese and potato 41
meat 43
sea bass: pan-fried sea bass with spices and Seville orange juice 193
stuffed sea bass with coriander, garlic and tamarind 191
Shirazi salad 51
spaghetti: Persian macaroni 209
spinach: beetroot with spinach and creamy yoghurt 31
fresh herb frittata with feta cheese 77
Persian noodle and herb soup 101
slow-cooked lamb with fresh herbs and beans 143
turnip soup with meat balls 93
yoghurt and chickpea soup 97
sumac 15

T
tahdig method, cooking rice 112–13
tamarind: cod with fresh herbs, garlic and tamarind 165
stuffed sea bass with coriander, garlic and tamarind 191
tomatoes: pan kebab with tomato and mushroom sauce 173

Persian macaroni 209
Persian meatballs in tomato and herb sauce 145–6
Persian omelette 79
Persian steak 181
Persian tomato soup 103
Shirazi salad 51
smoked aubergine with tomatoes, garlic and eggs 35
turnip soup with meatballs 93

W
walnuts: beef kebabs with pomegranate molasses, walnuts and herbs 179
caramelized nuts in leaf cups 65
chicken with walnuts and pomegranate molasses 161
crunchy walnut puffs 225
dates with crunchy walnuts and buttery cream 227
flower baklava with sticky syrup 229
goat's cheese with fresh herbs and walnuts 33
marinated olives with walnuts and mint 25
walnut, pistachio and almond muffins 223
watermelon, feta cheese and mint salad 61

Y
yellow split peas: lamb shanks with quince and prunes 155
yellow split peas with lamb 151–2
yoghurt: beetroot with spinach and creamy yoghurt 31
minty yoghurt drink 233
saffron yoghurt dressing 63
saffron yoghurt rice cupcakes 121
smoked aubergine with garlic and yoghurt 29
yoghurt and chickpea soup 97
yoghurt with cucumber, mint and dill 27

ROBINSON

First published in Great Britain in 2018 by Robinson

10 9 8 7 6 5 4 3 2 1

Copyright © Atoosa Sepehr, 2018

Photographs by Atoosa Sepehr

The moral right of the author has been asserted.

All rights reserved.

No part of this publication may be reproduced, stored in a retrieval system, or transmitted, in any form, or by any means, without the prior permission in writing of the publisher, nor be otherwise circulated in any form of binding or cover other than that in which it is published and without a similar condition including this condition being imposed on the subsequent purchaser.

A CIP catalogue record for this book is available from the British Library.

ISBN 978-1-47214-220-7

Designed by Atoosa Sepehr, Andrew Barron & Frank Winters

Printed and bound in Italy by L.E.G.O SpA

Papers used by Robinson are from well-managed forests and other responsible sources.

Robinson
An imprint of
Little, Brown Book Group
Carmelite House
50 Victoria Embankment
London EC4Y 0DZ

An Hachette UK Company

www.hachette.co.uk

www.littlebrown.co.uk

ACKNOWLEDGEMENTS

I would like to express my thanks to Frank Winters who developed the first iteration of the book design. I would also like to thank my agent Rachel Mills at Furniss Lawton for believing in me and for giving me guidance and encouragement. Lastly, I would like to extend my gratitude to all of the amazing team at Robinson (Little, Brown) for their wonderful support and for making my dream of publishing a Persian cookbook come true.